AF811914

# Shrink to Human

## Customer Experience in a World Built for Scale, Not People

Dennis Wakabayashi
THE GLOBAL VOICE OF CX

Shrink to Human
Customer Experience in a World Built for Scale, Not People



O'Donnell Publishing

ISBN 978-1-7330736-6-0

Contributing authors:
Ladislau Batalha, Gregório Uglioni, Camila Ferreira, Cristiani Oliveira

*This book is dedicated to Linda Zinda,*
*who asked me to make the world a better place.*

# Contents

INTRODUCTION

# The World Was Built to Scale. The Customer Still Decides as a Human.

I have spent my life listening to people inside systems.

In Dubai I sat with government ministers trying to understand why citizens were leaving public services feeling worse than when they arrived. In Johannesburg I sat with contact center agents taking three hundred calls a shift for companies with no mechanism to hear what those agents were learning. In São Paulo, executives could see customer trust eroding in their numbers while struggling to name what was moving.

Every conversation was different. The condition underneath was always the same.

People want to be understood. They want systems that respect their time and keep their promises. They want the effort they put into a relationship to mean something. That desire stays. What changed is how far systems have scaled beyond their ability to honor it.

The world learned how to scale systems faster than it learned how to understand people.

Platforms scale. Supply chains scale. AI answers scale. The infrastructure of commerce has become extraordinarily good at processing transactions at speeds most organizations are still learning to manage. A customer trusts through moments. Scale belongs to the company. Dignity comes from how the system treats them when something goes wrong, when they are confused, when they are deciding whether the company still deserves their confidence.

A person experiences a brand as a promise kept or broken. A clear answer or a runaround. A moment where the company made the next step easier, or one where it asked them to take on more than they should.

Customer Experience lives in those moments. For years organizations treated it as a service function. Then the practice matured: CX became a growth lever, a leadership priority, a financial discipline. That movement was necessary. It helped executives see what had always been true: loyalty, retention, and reputation are shaped by experience.

The world kept moving.

The customer relationship now exists in places most organizations miss. A prospect may stay outside the CRM, yet already have a belief about the brand. A lost customer may have stopped buying, yet still shape what the market expects. An AI answer may define the company before the company has a chance to speak.

To lead in this world means staying close enough to the person inside the system to understand what they are experiencing before the report does. Close enough to see the customer trying to trust. The employee trying to do good work. The leader trying to understand what is moving before the numbers explain it.

I call that practice shrinking to human. This book is built around it.

It is written for leaders who know CX is more than a department, who know trust takes more than technology alone, and who believe the future belongs to those who see it first: belief before behavior, customer evidence before the dashboard, and the practice before consensus arrives.

### What This Book Will Help Leaders See

The customer often reveals the truth before the company has a place to record it. Someone writes a review. Someone searches a question they are embarrassed to ask out loud. Someone makes a quiet decision to stop recommending a product they once trusted. The leader's task is to read those signals without turning them into noise.

Throughout this book I refer to ATLAS³. It is an intelligence platform I built to apply the evidence discipline these chapters describe. It reads customer language, search behavior, and AI answer results across the populations most organizations miss. The ideas work without it. Any organization that reads customer language with discipline is already doing this work. ATLAS³ is one way to do it at scale. The method belongs to you regardless.

What changes when you apply this discipline is the question you lead with.

| Old question | Better question |
|---|---|
| "How did we score?" | "What is moving, why is it moving, and what decision should we make while we still have time to improve the condition?" |

That question matters because the customer relationship is alive. Belief moves. Trust moves. Competitor meaning moves. The strongest leaders learn to read that movement before it appears as a business result.

They know customer experience is more than what the company delivers. It is what people come to believe about what the company delivers, how that belief spreads, and whether it changes decisions.

This work is practical, measurable, and teachable. It begins with the human layer. It begins with belief.

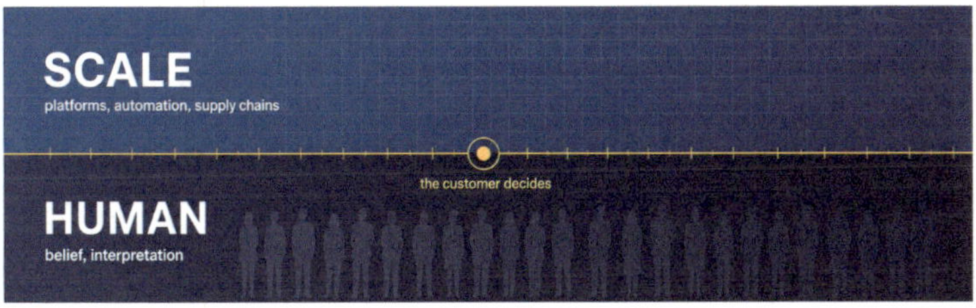


**Figure I.1** Scale layer over human layer.

Systems scale through infrastructure. Experience forms through human interpretation.

The chapters ahead show why belief is the smallest unit of experience, how customer language reveals operating pressure, and how AI answer results have become a new front door for the market's first impression of a brand.

They return to the core frameworks: the 3Rs of Reputation, Reach, and Relationships; the 4Es of Economic, Efficient, Emotional, and Empathetic experience; and the archetype pathways that give practitioners a professional map.

Customer Experience at scale becomes strongest when leaders keep human belief at the center of design, measurement, and execution.

---

*Shrink to Human.*

PART ONE

# The World Built for Scale

CHAPTER ONE

# Belief Forms Before the Company Sees the Customer

Customer Experience changed because the customer's world changed first.

For years, a company knew a customer when the customer showed up. A call came in. A survey went out. A renewal happened or it lapsed. Each of those moments created a record, and the record became the relationship. The company saw the customer when the customer was present.

The customer stopped waiting to be present.

Before a buyer calls, they have already read the reviews, compared the alternatives, and consulted an AI answer about which option is easier to leave. By the time the company sees that customer, a belief is already in place. It may show up as confidence, or as hesitation that survives onboarding.

Customer Experience needs a new operating logic because the old one assumed the relationship started when the company noticed it.

The customer's actual path now moves through search results, peer conversations, AI answer results, and the proof that surrounds the brand in places beyond the company's control, places it may overlook entirely. A prospect may stay outside the CRM, yet already have a firm opinion. A competitor's customer may be describing a switching window the sales team misses. An AI answer result may be shaping first impressions at scale, every day, invisibly.

Scale changed the customer's world first. CX must learn to see the customer inside that scaled world.

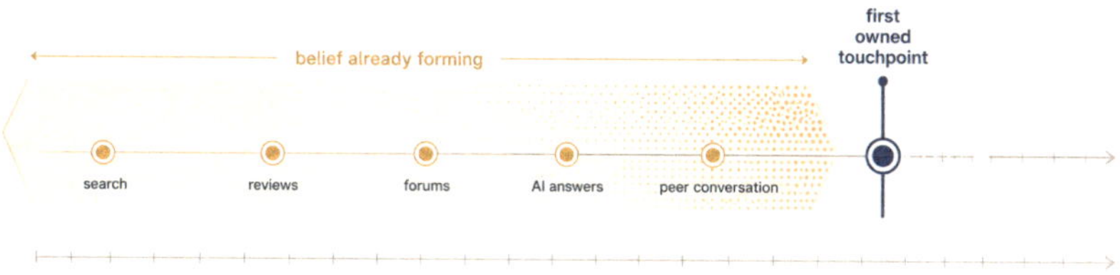


**Figure 1.1** Belief forms before the first touchpoint.

The customer may already have a belief before the first owned touchpoint.

## The Human Layer Inside Scale

The customer still decides as a human.

Platforms can organize access. Algorithms can filter options. AI answers can compress information. What stays the same is the moment a person decides whether a company deserves their confidence.

A company feels reliable or unreliable. A promise feels fair or unfair. A support experience restores confidence or leaves the customer with doubt. These judgments form through small signals: a confusing price page creates hesitation, a clear answer creates relief, an employee with the authority to solve the problem creates dignity for both sides of the interaction.

That is the human layer of Customer Experience. It is where business value begins.

When people believe the system will help them, they continue. When they believe the company understands what they are trying to accomplish, they are easier to retain, to serve, and to grow with.

The challenge in modern CX is that the system often reads the process before it reads the person. A dashboard may show activity while the person is living with effort. A score may show satisfaction while the person already feels doubt. The numbers can be correct and still miss what is moving.

I ask leaders to shrink attention down to the person inside the system. The metrics are accurate. They arrive after the belief has already formed. The strongest systems are designed by people who understand what a customer needs to believe in order to take the next step with confidence.

### CX as the Operating System

CX is the connective tissue of the business. It connects functions that were built to optimize separately. Marketing sets an expectation. Finance determines whether it feels fair. Operations decides whether it lasts. The frontline makes it human where the system falls short. The customer experiences all of that as a single relationship. The company usually experiences it as separate work.

That distance is where modern CX leadership begins.

Every function shapes what the customer comes to believe:

| Function | How it shapes belief |
|---|---|
| Product | Sets expectations through usability and delivered value |
| Marketing | Sets expectations through language and promise |
| Sales | Builds trust before purchase |
| Service | Protects trust through recovery |
| Finance | Shapes fairness through pricing and billing clarity |
| Operations | Creates reliability through consistency |
| HR | Builds employee readiness to deliver the experience |
| Technology | Shapes the conditions under which employees and customers move |
| Frontline | Makes the system human at the moment it matters most |

CX converts hierarchy into matrix. A hierarchy organizes authority. A matrix organizes responsibility. One asks who owns the function. The other asks whether the customer can move through the system with confidence. Customer Experience becomes structural when every function shares responsibility for what the customer comes to believe.

## What the Scaled System Can Learn to See

The customer's evidence lives across more places than traditional CX systems were designed to track. Reading that evidence is a discipline more than a technology. The discipline is this: look beyond the populations you are already measuring, and ask what the people outside your measurement are teaching the market.

The same signal reads differently depending on who is sending it. When a current customer says a product is getting harder to use, that is an adoption signal. When a prospect says it before buying, that is an acquisition barrier. When a competitor's customer says it about their current provider, that may be a window. Knowing which is which changes what you do next.

Tools like ATLAS[3] apply this reading at scale. The approach is available to any organization willing to look: separate who is speaking, note when, watch what repeats. Applied consistently, it lets leaders see where belief is forming before it shows up as stalled pipeline, higher cost-to-serve, or reduced trust continuity.

What this reading reveals is interpretation. A billing complaint is also a fairness question. A support delay is also a competence signal. A confusing AI answer is also a first impression. The evidence points to a belief, and the belief points to a system condition that can be improved.

Dashboards tell leaders what the company has already structured to measure. Customer evidence outside the dashboard tells leaders what the customer is already using to form belief. The stronger organization connects both.

| Customer evidence | What it reveals | Leadership question |
|---|---|---|
| Search questions | What buyers are unsure about before they buy | What must be made clearer? |
| Reviews | Which lived experiences have become proof for others | Which proof is shaping belief? |
| Forum posts | What peers teach one another about the brand | Which warnings or workarounds are spreading? |
| AI answer results | How machines summarize and compare the brand | Are we ignored, mentioned, compared, preferred, or defaulted? |
| Complaints | Where friction becomes visible | Which condition created the burden? |
| Competitor comparisons | Where switching becomes thinkable | Which belief gives the competitor an advantage? |
| Employee escalation patterns | Where the internal system strains | What must change so employees can help better? |
| Quiet exits | Where belief moved without direct explanation | What evidence appeared before the exit? |

## Reading Upstream

The question that changes the conversation is: where did the customer form belief before we saw them?

Most organizations start with questions the company can already answer: how many tickets closed, what the score was, what the dashboard showed. Those questions help leaders manage known systems. The discipline that creates an advantage starts upstream, before the company's measurement begins.

Every monthly CX review should include evidence from outside the dashboard. Keep it short. A structured conversation about what customers, prospects, lost customers, and AI answer results are teaching the market. The review should identify the belief forming and the evidence shaping it, the function able to improve the condition, and the proof that will show whether belief is moving in the right direction.

Scale changed the customer before CX changed itself. The work now is to make scale more intelligent by keeping the person visible inside it.

---

*That is how Customer Experience earns its place as an operating system across the business.*

CHAPTER TWO

# The Smallest Unit of Experience Is Belief

Customer Experience begins before the customer acts. It begins when the customer forms belief.

Consider two vendors with nearly identical products and nearly identical pricing. The buyer chooses the one that answered her email within an hour. Speed created the belief she was actually choosing: this company will be there when something goes wrong. The other vendor never knew they lost her, on a signal outside their measurement.

That is what makes belief the smallest unit of experience. It is smaller than a journey, smaller than a touchpoint, smaller than a score. It is the meaning underneath the behavior the company eventually measures. A dashboard may show what the customer did. Belief explains why.

A person can buy, complain, or leave. Each action creates data. The action is almost always the end of a story that started earlier. By the time the company sees the behavior, the belief that caused it has been in place for weeks.

Belief moved first.

The customer believed the company would help. The customer believed the process would be fair. The customer believed the brand understood their situation well enough to deserve trust. Or they believed something else. The experience confirmed the belief that was already there.

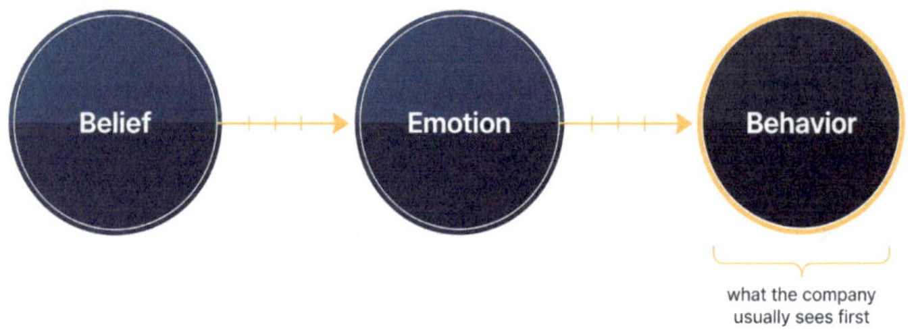


**Figure 2.1** Belief to behavior.

Customer action becomes easier to understand when leaders read the belief that came before it.

### What People Feel Before They Act

People experience companies as confidence, effort, and trust. The process map is the company's view.

A customer says, "This is taking too long." A customer says, "This feels unfair." A customer says nothing and begins looking somewhere else. The phrase "touchpoint three to touchpoint four" belongs to the company.

That is belief becoming language. It shows up through patience when something goes wrong, through forgiveness that can only be withdrawn once, and through resistance when the company asks for one more step, one more form, or one more wait. The company and the customer are often reading the same moment in entirely different ways:

| The company sees | The customer feels |
|---|---|
| A service case | A test of trust |
| A policy | A judgment about fairness |
| An automated message | Absence |

This is where many CX systems become too thin. They capture the visible event but under-read the state underneath it.

Satisfaction has value. It gives customers a formal voice inside the organization, and in companies that have long ignored customers, that matters. Satisfaction and belief are different. A customer can report satisfaction and still feel little attachment. A customer can give a high score and still switch when a better alternative feels safer or easier. Satisfaction tells leaders how a customer responded to a measured moment. Belief tells leaders what the customer is prepared to do next.

## Why Belief Matters to Leadership

I have become less interested in whether a customer says they are satisfied and more interested in what the experience makes them believe next. That is where leadership becomes sharper.

When belief is strong, customers give the company more room. They try again, forgive a mistake, and trust the company to make the situation right.

When belief is weak, customers narrow the relationship. They compare alternatives, interpret friction as evidence, and begin to protect themselves from the company they are still technically using.

The same operational event means different things depending on the belief state around it. A delayed order can be forgiven when the customer believes the company is honest and competent. The same delay creates anger when the customer already believes the company hides information. A chatbot feels useful when the customer believes it helps them move faster. The same chatbot feels dismissive when the customer believes the company is avoiding human responsibility.

Belief changes the meaning of the moment. Metrics tell leaders where something registered. Belief tells leaders what the registration meant.

The next generation of CX measurement needs a way to understand customer emotion in relation to the brand's actual promise. A bank needs to create confidence. A healthcare provider needs to create safety. A software platform needs to create momentum. A generic satisfaction score flattens those differences. A customer emotion score makes the goal legible to the people who shape the experience every day.

That is the leadership value of belief. It turns CX from a response system into a meaning system.

### Reading Belief Movement

Belief moves. It forms, strengthens, and weakens. It can be built through consistent delivery and eroded through repeated effort. A single complaint stays a single complaint. A repeated pattern begins to teach leaders what customers are coming to believe.

When customers repeatedly ask whether a product is worth it, belief about value is moving. When reviews repeatedly mention confusion, belief about ease is moving. When employees escalate the same issue week after week, belief inside the organization is moving too: the people closest to the customer begin to believe the system blocks them from helping the customer.

Reading that movement requires separating complaint language from decision language. Complaint language describes a burden. Decision language shows a customer preparing to act differently. They often sound similar. They mean different things:

| Language type | What it signals | Leadership response |
|---|---|---|
| "This was frustrating." | Burden. The customer may still want recovery. | Offer resolution. |
| "I am looking for another provider." | Decision. The customer is preparing to act. | Understand the belief driving the move. |
| "Use your points before they lose value." | Extraction. Value preservation before exit. | Look for quiet exit behavior. |

This discipline is available through structured listening programs, research teams, and analytics tools. ATLAS[3] applies it at scale. The principle is the same regardless of the instrument: make belief observable through the evidence people leave behind, and read it before the business outcome makes the cause irrelevant.

Belief becomes useful when leaders connect what people say to the state underneath it and the action it calls for.

| Customer says | Likely belief state | Leadership reading |
|---|---|---|
| "Is this worth it?" | Value is uncertain | Clarify economic value and proof. |
| "I don't know what happens next." | Confidence is weak | Reduce confusion in the journey. |
| "They make this easy." | Trust is forming | Protect the process that creates ease. |
| "This feels unfair." | Fairness is at risk | Review pricing, policy, or treatment. |
| "Who is better than this?" | Switching is thinkable | Understand the competing belief. |
| Silence after repeated effort | Relationship energy is declining | Look for quiet exit behavior. |

The goal is to read for pattern. Single phrases pass. Repeated language begins to organize around a belief. When the pattern is there, behavior follows.

## Adding the Belief Question

Add one question to every CX review: what did this experience make the customer believe?

Most reviews ask what happened. The stronger question reaches one level deeper, into the belief the experience created rather than the event it recorded. That shift changes the conversation. A support leader asks whether the customer left with confidence rather than whether the case closed. A product leader asks whether the experience created trust in continued use rather than whether adoption is up. A finance leader asks whether the process felt fair rather than whether payment completed.

The review should separate three states: belief forming, where the customer is gaining confidence; belief weakening, where doubt or effort is increasing; and belief moving, where the customer's interpretation is changing direction.

The leader who can see those states has more room to act before the dashboard confirms what the customer already knew.

---

*Belief comes before behavior. Every system that misses this is measuring outcomes while the causes are already somewhere else.*

CHAPTER THREE

# The Matrix Organization

A customer rarely knows who owns the billing system. They only know that the explanation on the website differs from what the service team told them, and that the third person they have now spoken to is still looking for what the second person wrote down.

That experience came from several departments succeeding on their own terms.

This is the organizational problem Customer Experience was built to solve. The customer experiences the company as a single relationship. The company experiences the customer as separate work belonging to separate functions. Marketing owns the promise. Service owns the recovery. Finance owns the terms. The customer lives in the seam between them.

CX converts hierarchy into matrix. A hierarchy organizes authority: it tells people who controls what. A matrix organizes responsibility: it asks whether the customer can move through the full system with confidence. The shift matters because belief follows the experience. The org chart matters less.

When a product is hard to use, trust moves. When a bill is unclear, trust moves. When every team works from a different definition of success, the customer feels the seams. A modern CX organization exists to remove them.

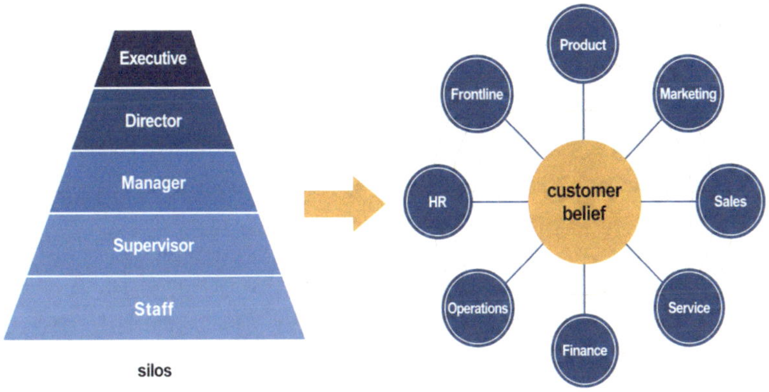


**Figure 3.1** Hierarchy becomes a matrix.

CX becomes structural when every function shares responsibility for the customer's belief.

### The Human Problem Inside the Org Chart

Most organizations were designed around control, specialization, and accountability rather than the customer's lived path. Those needs are real. The problem begins when the structure becomes more visible to the customer than the experience.

The customer can feel the handoff. They feel it when the website makes one promise and the service team explains a different reality. They feel it when billing, onboarding, and recovery were clearly built by teams that worked independently from each other. At that point the customer takes on work that belongs inside the company: translating the company to itself. They explain the same issue more than once. They bring context from one channel to the next. They learn the internal limits of the organization by experiencing them.

Employees feel the same strain from the other side. A frontline worker hears the customer's frustration while the policy that caused it stays outside their reach. A service leader sees repeat contacts while the source of the issue stays outside their authority. A finance leader protects short-term revenue while the trust cost grows downstream.

Most of these people are trying to do good work. The system rewards local optimization. Good people create fragmented experiences when the structure asks them to win separately.

CX leadership changes the question. Instead of asking whether each function performed well on its own terms, it asks whether the customer could move through the full system with confidence.

### Belief Before Title

Many organizations try to solve this by assigning a title. A Chief Customer Officer, Chief Experience Officer, or senior CX leader can create visibility, language, and focus. Belief comes from somewhere else.

Without the belief that CX belongs across the business, the title becomes symbolic. The leader may own a dashboard and a voice-of-customer program, but the operating system remains unchanged. The work still depends on the same silos that created the problem.

Top-down CX implementation underperforms when the order arrives before the belief does. The experience lives in the middle and at the frontline. Middle managers translate strategy into daily work. Frontline managers decide whether employees receive the feedback, tools, and permission needed to help the customer. Both groups move when the work earns their trust. An announcement rarely moves them.

CX moves when enough people believe the work belongs to them.

Product leaders can be powerful CX owners because they already live across use, adoption, and friction. They work with design, engineering, marketing, sales, and support. When they understand belief, they become natural matrix leaders because they already operate where customer value has to become real. The same is true of strong operators and commercial leaders. The title matters less than the ability to move across the system and create shared responsibility.

One influential leader matters. The matrix needs a person who can set direction, simplify the work, and create enough trust for others to move. Committees coordinate. They rarely move belief. A strong leader gives the system a center of gravity without having to own every action.

The CX expert brings the toolkit and the diagnosis. The operating leader shapes the larger share because the experience has to live inside daily work. Implementation succeeds in co-creation and fails in hand-off. When belief reaches the middle manager layer, CX stops being an initiative. It becomes how the company works.

### How the Matrix Protects the Customer

A matrix organization protects the customer by making belief a shared operating responsibility. Functional ownership stays. The matrix gives each function a clearer relationship to what the customer comes to believe.

| Function | What the matrix asks of it |
|---|---|
| Marketing | Shape expectations the business can actually fulfill |
| Product | Create usable value, not only ship features |
| Sales | Build trust that the delivered experience will match the sold one |
| Service | Restore confidence, not only resolve tickets |
| Finance | Protect fairness through pricing, billing, and term clarity |
| Operations | Protect reliability through consistency |
| HR | Build the conditions that allow employees to serve with clarity and dignity |
| Technology | Make work easier for the people who use it |
| Frontline | Make the system human at the moment it matters most |

When these functions move together, the customer feels coherence. Coherence creates confidence. Confidence creates trust. Trust creates continuity.

Reading where belief is moving across that system is how the matrix stays honest. If customers repeat language about confusion, the matrix can ask whether the source is product, marketing, onboarding, or policy. If employees escalate the same issue week after week, it can ask which internal condition is producing external friction. The purpose is to locate the condition that can be improved. Blame stays out of the discussion.

### Customer Belief Responsibility Map

Mapping each function's contribution to belief makes the matrix practical rather than aspirational.

| Function | Primary contribution to belief | Leadership question |
| --- | --- | --- |
| Product | Makes the promise usable | Does the product help the customer succeed with less effort? |
| Marketing | Sets expectations | Are we creating belief the business can fulfill? |
| Sales | Builds pre-purchase trust | Are we selling the experience the customer will actually receive? |
| Service | Restores confidence | Does recovery leave the customer stronger than before the issue? |
| Finance | Shapes fairness | Do pricing, billing, and terms feel clear and honest? |
| Operations | Creates reliability | Can the customer count on the system to work consistently? |
| HR | Builds employee readiness | Are employees equipped to deliver the experience we promise? |
| Technology | Enables access and judgment | Does the tool make the work simpler, clearer, and more human? |
| Frontline | Makes the system human | Can the employee act with clarity, authority, and dignity? |

The stronger matrix asks every team to understand the CX meaning of the work they already do. The volume of work stays the same.

### Three Moves

Add one question to every functional review already on the calendar: how did this function strengthen or weaken customer belief?

That question belongs in every functional review. In a product review, leaders ask whether the experience is becoming easier to use. In a finance review, whether the customer experiences value and fairness. In an HR review, whether employees have the clarity, tools, and authority required to deliver. The question belongs inside the operating rhythm.

Three moves make this practical. First, add the belief question to every functional review. Second, treat the middle manager layer as the layer where the work actually happens. Give them trust, context, and a clear reason to believe the CX work will make their teams stronger rather than add another reporting burden. Third, choose one influential operating leader to build the work with CX as a partner: someone with enough trust to move across functions and enough humility to co-create with the people closest to the customer.

Hierarchy becomes matrix when the customer stops feeling the seams, the employee shares the burden across the system, and every function can see the belief condition it helps create.

---

*That is the structure belief requires.*

PART TWO

# Deciphering Customer Experience

CHAPTER FOUR

# Customer Evidence Outside the Dashboard

The customer often teaches the market before the company sees the lesson.

In 2023 a mid-sized software company watched its trial-to-paid conversion rate fall for three consecutive quarters. The dashboard showed healthy engagement. Support tickets were down. Satisfaction scores stayed flat. Every internal signal said the product was fine.

What the dashboard missed was happening in a community forum. Users were posting workarounds. Not complaints: workarounds. Step-by-step instructions for getting around a part of the product that confused them, written by customers who had long stopped expecting the company to fix it. New users were finding the forum before they found the official help center. The belief forming around the product was being written by people the company had never measured.

The customer relationship lives both inside the systems a company builds to contain it and in the places where people decide what to believe before the company can measure them.

### The Customer Looks for Proof Before Commitment

Customers form belief from whatever helps them decide. The company's preferred feedback channel is one option among many.

They read the review that sounds like their situation. They search the question they are embarrassed to ask out loud. They trust the peer who is just another customer. For the customer this is a quiet search for confidence, and it may happen long before the company knows a decision is being made.

The company may believe it is listening because it has dashboards full of data. The customer may be forming belief in places those dashboards miss. A survey tells the company what a respondent said after a measured interaction. A forum thread shows the workaround customers built when they stopped expecting a solution. An AI answer shows how the wider evidence environment is being compressed into a recommendation the system produced, one the company may have yet to see.

Most companies have more data than they can use well. The problem is that the customer's decision path spreads across sources, communities, and answer systems partly outside the company's control. Listening must expand without becoming noise. The goal is to identify the evidence shaping belief rather than collect everything.

## The Unknown Customer Shapes the Market Too

CX leaders need to know who the company is actually hearing.

Most organizations hear primarily from known customers: people who bought, contacted support, or agreed to answer a survey. That is real evidence, but it is a narrow slice of the market. A prospect comparing options, a lost customer whose explanation keeps traveling, a competitor's customer looking for a reason to switch: all live outside managed data. All of them influence what the market comes to believe.

A prospect who stays outside the pipeline still affects acquisition if their question names a barrier many buyers share. A lost customer still affects retention if their explanation becomes the language others use to describe the brand. A competitor's customer still affects growth if their complaint reveals a switching window the sales team misses.

The work expands accordingly. The job is to improve measured interactions and to understand how belief forms around the company, including in the places where the company stays absent. That requires discipline. Evidence and volume are different. A repeated search question is meaningful because it shows uncertainty before purchase. A forum thread is meaningful because it shows the workaround customers have normalized. A shift in how AI answers describe the brand is meaningful because it changes how buyers first encounter it.

Reading evidence with judgment is the skill. The leader's job is to connect the signal to the belief without overstating either.

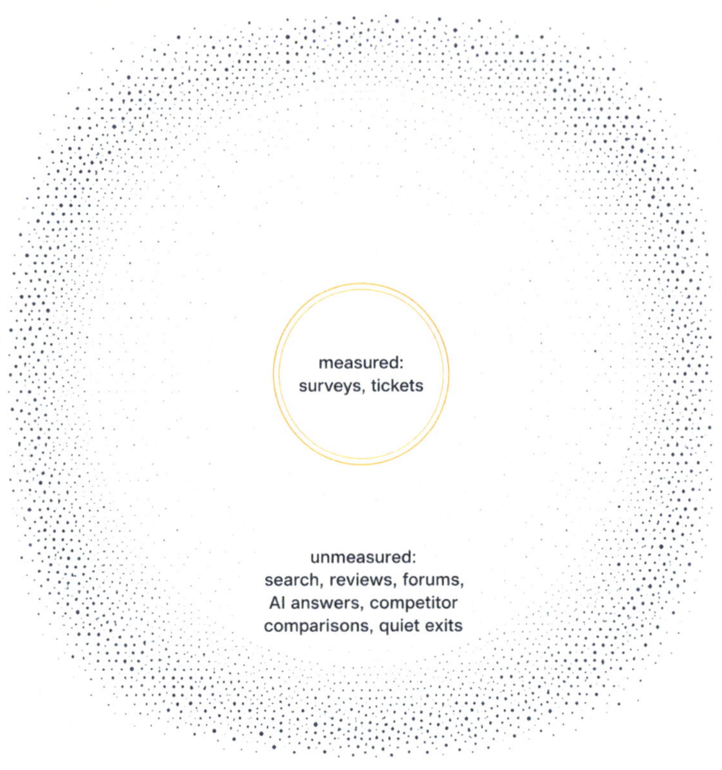


**Figure 4.1** Measured inside, unmeasured outside.

A company can miss most of the market conversation when it only measures people already inside its systems.

## Reading Evidence Across Populations

The same phrase means different things depending on who says it, when they say it, and how often it appears.

When a current customer says a product is getting harder to use, that is an adoption signal. When a prospect says it, that is an acquisition barrier. When a competitor's customer says it about their current provider, that may be a window. When AI answers begin repeating it, the phrase may be shaping first impressions at scale before any buyer has spoken to the company.

Timing matters as much as source. A complaint after a known service interruption means one thing. The same complaint rising steadily before a renewal cycle means something else. A search question appearing once after a pricing change may show confusion. The same question appearing across six months reveals a persistent value issue that the company has to address.

Recurrence is the third dimension. A single review stays a single review. A pattern across reviews begins to teach leaders what customers are coming to believe, and what they are telling each other. The phrase that repeats is the system speaking through the customer.

Tools like ATLAS[3] apply this reading at scale. The approach is available to any organization willing to look: separate who is speaking, note when, watch what repeats. Applied consistently, this creates the practical advantage of seeing where belief is forming before it appears as stalled pipeline, lower adoption, or reduced trust continuity.

Evidence outside the dashboard becomes useful when leaders connect each source to what it teaches and what action it supports.

| Evidence source | What it teaches | Leadership use |
|---|---|---|
| Search questions | What people need clarified before they commit | Improve language, proof, and buying guidance |
| Reviews | Which lived experiences are becoming proof for others | Protect strengths and correct recurring friction |
| Forum posts | How peers explain the brand when the company is absent | Identify workarounds, warnings, and shared belief |
| Competitor comparisons | Where customers see alternatives as stronger | Understand the belief advantage competitors hold |
| AI answer results | How machine-mediated answers summarize the brand | Improve retrievable proof and recommendation strength |
| Employee escalation patterns | Where the internal system creates customer burden | Remove process strain before it reaches the customer repeatedly |
| Quiet exits | Where belief moved without direct explanation | Find early evidence that appeared before the departure |

Each source must teach something. Each lesson must connect to a leadership use. That is how evidence becomes action rather than decoration.

## Building the Evidence Review

Build a regular evidence review that reaches beyond known customer data. Keep it short. A disciplined conversation, held monthly, about which evidence is shaping belief and which condition the organization can improve.

A strong review covers more than current customers. It asks what prospects, lost customers, competitor customers, employees, and AI answer results are each teaching the market. It identifies the belief forming and the evidence shaping it, the population using the language, and the function able to improve the condition and show whether it changed.

The software company eventually found the forum. They fixed the confusing flow. Conversion recovered over the following two quarters. The fix took three weeks. Finding the signal took three years because the habit of looking outside the dashboard had to be built.

---

*The organization becomes better at seeing by reading the evidence that shapes belief rather than by collecting more.*

CHAPTER FIVE

# Customer Language Reveals Operational Pressure

At a subscription software company, the phrase "how do I cancel" appeared in support transcripts about once a week in January. By June it was appearing seventeen times a week. No alert had fired. Nobody had been counting it. The word "cancel" appeared in records categorized under a different label, and that category was reporting as stable.

Cancellations were visible in the dashboard. What they missed was the signal: customers were searching for the exit months before they took it. The language was telling them something three or four months ahead of the churn event. They were reading the outcome. The cause was still visible in the words.

That is what customer language does. When enough people repeat the same phrase, they are describing a system condition rather than expressing sentiment. They are naming the place in the operation where the experience is asking too much.

A single phrase can be noise. A repeated phrase is different. Repetition shows that more than one person is using the same words to describe the same condition. That condition may live in product design, pricing, onboarding, or the distance between what the company promised and what the customer received.

When customers keep saying "hard to cancel," the issue may be more than cancellation. It may be trust, fairness, or perceived friction. When customers keep asking whether something is "worth it," the issue may be more than price. It may be value clarity. When customers keep comparing the brand to a competitor, the issue may be belief transfer.

The language points to the system.

### The Human Meaning Inside Repeated Words

Customers rarely describe experience in the language companies use to manage it. The distance between those two vocabularies is where the signal lives.

| The company calls it | The customer says |
|---|---|
| Activation flow | "I cannot get started." |
| Self-service | "I cannot find a human." |
| Retention offer | "They only cared when I tried to leave." |

The customer's words are closer to the lived experience than the company's internal language. They show the practical and emotional work the customer is doing: confusion, effort, doubt, comparison. And they often appear before the behavior becomes visible in a dashboard.

A customer may search "how hard is it to cancel" months before the cancellation event. A buyer may ask "is this still worth it" before conversion slows. An employee may say "we keep hearing the same issue" before leadership classifies the process as broken. The phrase is close to belief. The person is reporting a problem and revealing how the experience is being interpreted.

A customer who says "this feels unfair" is evaluating the company's intent. A customer who says "there has to be a better option" is already opening the door to comparison. A customer who says nothing after repeated effort may be moving toward quiet exit. The strongest CX leaders ask what the words are trying to teach rather than sorting them into positive or negative sentiment.

## Why Language Belongs in Leadership Decisions

Customer language belongs in leadership decisions because it names the conditions beneath the metrics.

A metric may show conversion slowing. Language can show that buyers do not understand the offer. A metric may show support volume rising. Language can show that the same confusing step is forcing customers to ask for help. A metric may show satisfaction staying steady. Language can show that confidence is weakening in the populations the survey never reached.

Language belongs above the chart. It should help explain the chart.

If customers repeat "I do not know what to do next," the issue may be onboarding clarity. If they repeat "support was kind but could not help," the issue may be employee authority. If they repeat "AI says they are not the best option," the issue may be proof quality outside the company's owned content. In each case the language locates the condition more precisely than the metric does.

Language also protects leaders from solving the wrong problem. A company may treat low satisfaction as a service training issue when the language shows a pricing fairness issue. It may treat weak adoption as a product education issue when the language shows that customers question the feature's value. The metric points to a symptom. The language points to the cause.

That is why repeated language deserves a place in the operating rhythm. Every function gains a shared way to understand what the customer is actually experiencing.

### Reading the Language, Not Just the Score

Reading customer language as a management discipline requires separating three dimensions: movement, source, and type.

Movement shows whether a phrase is increasing or fading. A phrase that appears twice a month in January and forty times a month in June is telling a different story than one that stays steady. Source shows where the language appears and who is producing it. A current customer saying a product is confusing is an adoption signal. A prospect saying it is an acquisition barrier. A lost customer saying it is a memory that still shapes reputation. The same phrase means different things depending on who says it.

Type is the third dimension: complaint language describes a burden, while decision language shows a customer preparing to act differently. They often sound similar but they call for different responses:

| Language type | What it signals | Leadership response |
|---|---|---|
| "This was frustrating." | Burden. Customer may still want recovery. | Offer resolution. |
| "I am looking for another provider." | Decision. Customer is preparing to act. | Understand the belief driving the move. |
| "I used to recommend them." | Trust movement. Advocacy is cooling. | Identify what changed in proof or delivery. |

Tools like ATLAS[3] apply this reading across populations, time periods, and channels simultaneously. The discipline is available to any organization willing to look: track what repeats, note who is saying it, and separate the burden from the decision. Language analysis stays simple. The purpose is to make customer reality harder to miss.

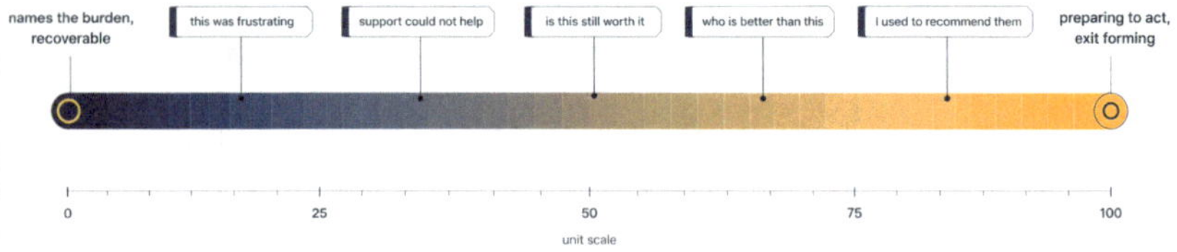


**Figure 5.1** From complaint to decision language.

Complaint language names the burden. Decision language shows the customer preparing to act.

Repeated customer language becomes useful when leaders connect the phrase to the belief underneath it and the system condition it may be describing.

| Repeated customer language | Belief underneath | Likely system condition | Action |
|---|---|---|---|
| "I don't know what happens next." | Journey lacks clarity | Onboarding, communication, or handoff confusion | Simplify the next step and make ownership visible. |
| "This feels unfair." | Trust in intent is weakening | Pricing, policy, billing, or exception handling | Review fairness, transparency, and recovery logic. |
| "Support was kind but couldn't help." | Employees lack authority | Frontline enablement or escalation limits | Give employees clearer decision rights. |
| "Is this still worth it?" | Value confidence is weakening | Proof, pricing, adoption, or outcome clarity | Reconnect value to the customer's goal. |
| "Who is better than this?" | Switching is thinkable | Competitor belief advantage | Understand what the alternative now represents. |
| "I used to recommend them." | Advocacy is cooling | Trust continuity weakening | Identify what changed in proof, delivery, or relationship. |

The table is a reading discipline, not a script. When the phrase points to clarity, improve clarity. When it points to authority, improve the employee's ability to act. When it points to comparison, understand what the competitor now owns in the customer's mind.

### Putting Language Into the Operating Review

The practice is simple. Each monthly operating review should include a small set of repeated customer phrases, qualified by source, population, and recurrence. Not a page of quotes. Not emotional color. Evidence of system conditions.

The leadership team asks what the phrase reveals, which belief is underneath it, which part of the system may be producing it, and what action would change the condition. Product hears the language of usability. Finance hears the language of fairness. Service hears the language of recovery. Executives hear the language of trust movement.

When the organization hears the customer in the customer's words, the work becomes harder to misunderstand. A complaint becomes more than dissatisfaction. A search phrase becomes more than curiosity. A quiet phrase becomes an early sign of what the customer may do next.

The subscription company eventually built that habit. A customer language register, reviewed monthly, with ownership assigned to each repeated phrase. Within two quarters they had identified three system conditions they had been misattributing to service quality for over a year.

---

*The language had been there the whole time. Nobody had been reading it.*

CHAPTER SIX

# The Quiet Exit

A regional bank lost fourteen thousand customers in a single quarter. The churn looked sudden on the report. When the team pulled the data, the exits clustered around a product change from eight months earlier: the bank had simplified its app by removing a feature that a loyal segment used every week. No complaints had been filed. Support contacts had actually declined after the change. The customers had quietly stopped believing the bank was built for them, and they had quietly found somewhere else to go.

From inside the company, the exit almost always builds slowly. From inside the customer, it is a gradual withdrawal of belief.

A customer may still log in. They may still answer a survey with a neutral score. They may still appear active on the dashboard. Inside the relationship, something has already changed. They have stopped recommending. They are using what they already paid for without adding to it. They are becoming more careful with their time and attention.

Then one day the company sees the outcome. The cancellation. The missed renewal. The employee who hears a phrase that has been repeated for months: "I already moved on."

Churn is often the final record of a belief that moved much earlier. The customer leaves in stages: confidence weakens, effort begins to feel heavier than the relationship warrants, and an alternative starts to look safer than the work of staying.

A CX leader needs to see that movement early enough to do something about it.

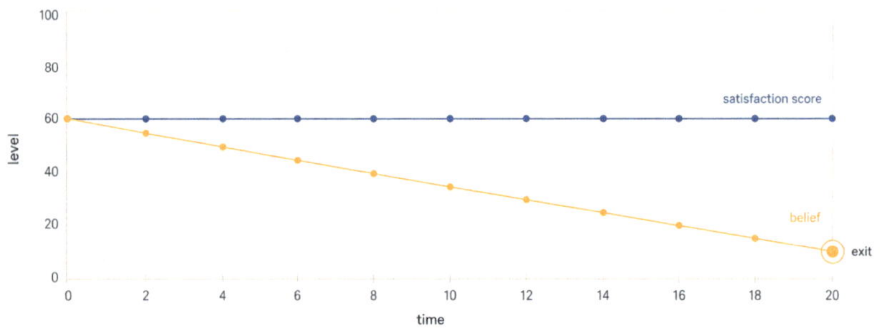


**Figure 6.1** Stable score, falling belief.

The score stays calm while the exit language begins moving outside the sample.

## The Customer Who Stops Explaining

Trust often changes before the customer says anything.

Some people complain because they still believe the company might respond. Some call because they still want resolution. Silence means something different. It can mean the customer has stopped expecting the company to understand. It can mean they have decided that improving the relationship costs more energy than it returns.

This makes the customer human. People have limited energy and they decide where to spend it. When a company repeatedly asks a customer to re-explain, wait, or work around the system, the customer eventually calculates whether the relationship still deserves that effort. That calculation may never appear as a complaint.

It appears as reduced use. Fewer recommendations. A support interaction that has become shorter and more transactional. Value extraction, where the customer uses what remains but stops investing belief.

The company may see activity. The person may be preparing to leave.

This is one of the most important differences between a metric and a belief state. A customer who is more active may be more loyal, or they may be using remaining value before moving on. A customer who contacts support less often may be more satisfied, or they may have stopped trying. A customer who gives a neutral score may be stable, or they may have stopped caring enough to give the company useful feedback.

The quiet exit asks leaders to read behavior with humility. The customer's silence means something. It may contain a decision.

### Satisfaction Is Part of the Relationship

Satisfaction scores helped CX earn attention inside companies. They gave customers a formal voice and helped executives see that experience deserved measurement. That value remains. The limitation appears when the organization treats the score as the whole picture.

At scale, satisfaction can stabilize in ways that give leaders a false sense of control. A customer may appreciate a polite employee and still believe the system behind that employee is too difficult to work with. A customer may complete a survey but avoid the next purchase. A customer may remain because leaving takes effort rather than because trust is growing.

A customer emotion score is more useful than a generic satisfaction score when it is tied to the brand's actual promise. A bank that promises simplicity should measure relief. A healthcare provider that promises safety should measure confidence. A platform that promises expertise should measure trust in judgment. The right measure makes the goal legible to every employee who shapes the experience, not just the team that reads the report.

The quiet exit often begins when the promised emotional state stops appearing. The customer may still be present. The belief is already moving.

## Reading Exit Before Exit

The discipline is to separate general frustration from decision movement. General frustration tells the organization that a customer is experiencing burden. Decision movement shows a customer preparing to act differently. They often arrive together but they call for entirely different responses.

A customer who says "this was difficult" may still be inviting recovery. A customer who says "I am looking for another option" is in a different state. A customer who says "use it before it loses value" is showing extraction behavior: they are taking what remains before they go. Reading which state a customer is in changes what the organization does next.

The evidence connecting these states to outcomes lives across more places than a single dashboard can show. A stable score can appear alongside rising departure language. Rising engagement can appear alongside falling fairness language. Positive service comments can appear alongside growing competitor comparison. These contradictions are the point of the analysis rather than problems in the data. The customer relationship is moving in more than one place simultaneously, and the company may be measuring only one of them.

Tools like ATLAS[3] read these intersections across language, time, and population. The approach is available through structured listening disciplines: track departure language separately from complaint language, watch where competitor comparisons are becoming specific, and note when employees begin escalating the same issue before the account data reflects it. The evidence for the quiet exit tends to appear earlier in language than it does in behavior.

The quiet exit becomes easier to see when leaders connect early evidence to the belief movement underneath it.

| Early evidence | Belief movement | Leadership reading |
|---|---|---|
| Customers search for alternatives | Staying feels less certain | Understand what the alternative represents. |
| Usage rises while trust language falls | Activity may reflect extraction | Check whether customers are deepening use or taking remaining value. |
| Support interactions become shorter or colder | Relationship energy is declining | Review whether the customer still expects help. |
| "Worth it" questions increase | Value confidence is weakening | Clarify proof, outcomes, and economic value. |
| Competitor comparisons become specific | Switching is becoming practical | Identify the belief advantage the competitor has. |
| Customers stop complaining after repeated effort | Recovery belief may be fading | Look for unresolved friction and silent exit behavior. |

The table is a reading discipline, not an alarm system. It asks leaders to notice when evidence begins to show a customer moving from repair to replacement. That movement deserves attention because it is still close enough to the experience to be improved.

## Measuring the Space Before the Exit

Most organizations study churn after it happens. They inspect the final account, review the last interaction, and look for the trigger. That work has value. It arrives late.

The stronger discipline is to study what appeared before the exit became official. What language changed first. What questions customers began asking. Which competitors entered the conversation and when. Which employees had been escalating the same condition for months before the account moved.

A quiet exit review, held monthly, should begin with early evidence: departure language, specific competitor comparisons, and value extraction patterns. Churn totals come later. The review asks which customers are leaving because the relationship no longer serves them, and which are leaving because the system made belief harder than it needed to be.

That distinction matters. It protects the business from chasing every retention outcome at the expense of clarity and fit. It protects employees from impossible expectations. And it protects customers from being treated as targets instead of people.

The bank eventually built that review. They discovered the feature removal. Eight months of exits had already happened. But they changed the process for how product decisions were evaluated against belief signals, and the quiet exit rate in the following year dropped by a third.

---

*Retention becomes more human by making the relationship worth continuing rather than by trapping customers.*

CHAPTER SEVEN

# AI Answer Results Are the New Front Door

Ask a language model which company in your category delivers the best customer service. Watch where your brand appears in the answer. Note what it says about you and what it leaves out. Note which competitors it describes with more confidence, and what language it uses to explain why.

Most CX leaders have yet to do this. Most cannot tell you where their brand stands in AI-mediated discovery, what evidence the answers are drawing from, or whether the position has shifted in the past six months.

This is the new front door. For most organizations, nobody owns it.

For years, companies controlled the first impression. The website, the store, the sales call, the search result: these were places the company could design, test, and improve. AI answer results add a different kind of entrance. A buyer asks which platform is easiest to leave. A patient asks which provider is most trusted. A small business owner asks which software has better support. The answer that shapes their belief is built from evidence the company did not write, delivered by a system the company does not control, before the customer has spoken to anyone in the organization.

AI answer results are now part of the customer experience because they influence what people believe before they choose, buy, call, compare, or leave.

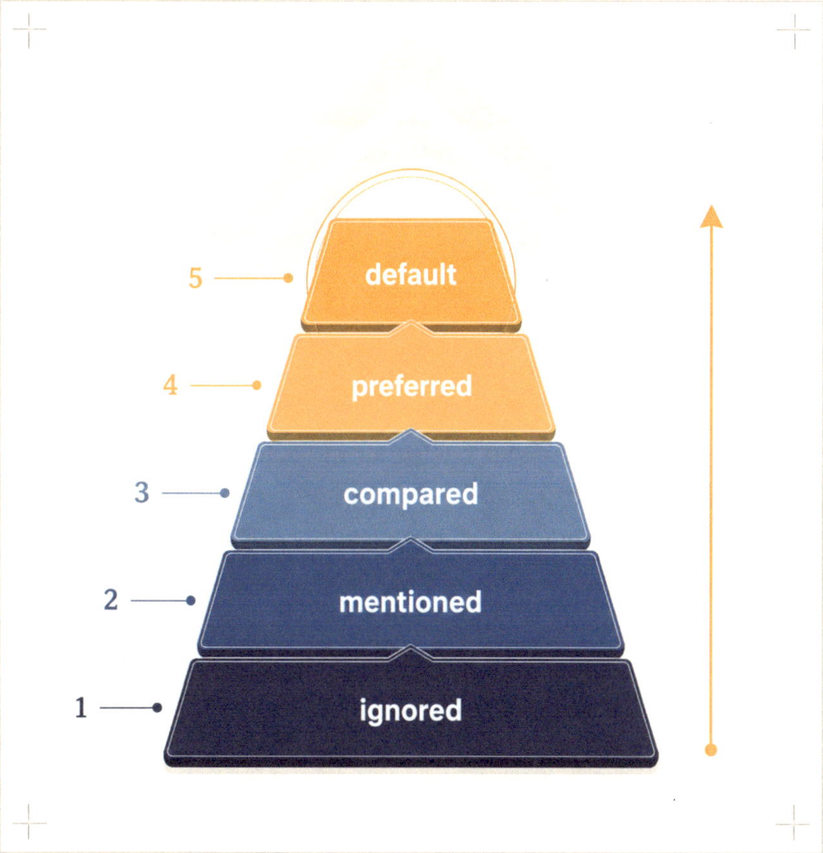


**Figure 7.1** The AI visibility ladder.

In AI-mediated discovery, the brand falls somewhere on a spectrum. It is ignored, mentioned, compared, preferred, or treated as the default.

## The Human Problem Inside AI Answers

Customers ask AI for help because decision-making has become heavy. There are too many options, too many claims, and too many promises that sound alike. An AI answer compresses that complexity into a shorter path to judgment.

That compression is useful to the customer and consequential for the brand. The answer gives the customer language. It frames the comparison. It may place one company beside another before the customer has visited either site. The customer has no simple way to know which evidence shaped the answer. They only experience the result.

A company can be visible in search and weak in AI answers. It can publish strong claims and still lack proof that answer systems can retrieve. It can improve its operations and still be described through older customer language because the evidence has not caught up to the experience. A company can have loyal customers and lose the first comparison if the retrievable proof is unclear.

The human question is direct: what does the customer believe after AI answers the question? That belief becomes part of the experience before the company has said a word.

### What AI Visibility Means for CX Leaders

AI visibility is different from awareness. Awareness means the customer has heard of the brand. AI visibility asks whether the brand appears with enough useful evidence to shape a decision. The difference between those two states is significant, and it maps to a spectrum:

| Position | What it means for the customer | What it means for the brand |
|---|---|---|
| Ignored | The brand is absent from the decision set | The customer may never consider the brand in this context |
| Mentioned | The brand appears with little explanation | Present but not persuasive |
| Compared | The brand is evaluated beside alternatives | In the decision set but proof may be weaker than competitors |
| Preferred | The brand earns recommendation with reasons | Evidence is strong enough to support a positive judgment |
| Default | The brand is the expected answer | The brand has become the obvious choice for this question |

AI systems retrieve and interpret available evidence rather than reward intent. A company may intend to be known for reliability, but the answer system will look for retrievable proof of reliability. It may intend to be known for ease, but if the forum posts describe workarounds, those posts are part of the evidence environment too.

The responsibility this creates is new. Leaders must make the experience true in the world, and then make the proof of that experience visible enough to be retrieved, trusted, and repeated. The company's AI position is shaped by the totality of what customers say about it, how competitors are described beside it, and how recently that evidence was created.

### Understanding Why the Position Is What It Is

Knowing where the brand stands is useful. Knowing why it stands there is what makes the information actionable.

The position may reflect weak or stale proof: the company has improved, but the retrievable evidence has not caught up. It may reflect stronger evidence from a competitor who has done a better job of making their customer outcomes visible and credible. It may reflect language the company has kept general, so the system describes the brand in general terms when a buyer is asking a specific question.

Each of those conditions requires a different response. Stale proof requires new retrievable evidence, not a content rewrite. Competitor advantage requires understanding what the competitor owns in the customer's mind, not just in the market. Unclear positioning requires clearer language tied to real customer outcomes, not broader claims.

Without that separation, organizations solve the wrong problem. They invest in more content when the issue is delivery proof. They increase paid visibility when the issue is trust. They rewrite messaging when the issue is the customer experience itself.

Tools like ATLAS[3] monitor AI answer results as part of the customer relationship, tracking position, evidence sources, and competitor language across time. The discipline is available to any organization willing to look: run the queries customers actually run, read what the answers say, and ask what evidence the system is drawing from. Do this regularly, not once.

AI visibility becomes actionable when leaders connect each position to its cause and the response it requires.

| Position | Likely cause | Leadership response |
|---|---|---|
| Ignored | No retrievable proof around the customer's question | Build clearer evidence around the decision the customer is making. |
| Mentioned | Brand is known but evidence is thin or generic | Strengthen specific outcome language and customer proof. |
| Compared | Evidence exists but competitors' is stronger | Identify the proof weakness that prevents preference. |
| Preferred | Evidence supports recommendation | Protect proof and keep it current; recency matters. |
| Default | Brand is the consistent answer for this question | Maintain trust, consistency, and fresh customer evidence. |

The goal is to focus on the answers that matter. A question about the best enterprise software for small accounting firms produces a different consequence than a generic brand mention. The leader's job is to identify which questions influence customer belief at meaningful decision moments, and to make sure the brand's position in those moments is built on accurate, current, retrievable proof.

## Taking Ownership of the Front Door

The practical starting point is to run the queries. Identify the five or six questions customers in your market actually ask when they are trying to choose, compare, trust, or avoid. Ask them. Read the answers carefully. Note the position, the evidence cited, and the competitors named with more confidence than your brand.

That reading becomes the input for a cross-functional conversation. Marketing can clarify the language that makes the brand easier to retrieve. Product and service can generate the outcome proof the answer system needs. Operations and finance can address the trust weaknesses that negative customer language reflects. None of this is a content strategy in the traditional sense. It is an experience strategy: make the truth retrievable.

The brands that earn the strongest AI positions are rarely the ones with the most content. They are the ones whose customers say the clearest things about them, whose proof is recent and specific, and whose experience has given the answer system something honest and credible to work with.

---

*AI answer results reveal what the evidence environment already says about a company. The question leaders need to answer goes deeper than improving the AI answer. It is whether the experience is strong enough to deserve a better one.*

CHAPTER EIGHT

# The Discipline of Experience Intelligence

A quarterly satisfaction score is a snapshot. It shows where things were at the moment the shutter clicked. It misses whether the customer who gave a seven is moving toward an eight or heading toward a three. It misses whether language outside the survey sample has begun organizing around a departure. It misses what that snapshot will look like in ninety days.

Experience intelligence is what happens when leaders start watching the film.

Trust moves. Belief moves. AI answer results move. The customer relationship is alive in more ways than a single score shows. Experience intelligence is the discipline of reading those movements together: looking beyond the measured surface to understand what is changing underneath, and making decisions based on direction rather than position.

A score may show stability while customer language begins to shift. Engagement may rise while fairness weakens. AI answers may keep the brand in comparison instead of preference while the search report shows visibility improving. Experience intelligence asks leaders to weigh all of those things at once, and to read the distance between what the company is measuring and what the customer is actually living.

### People Change Before Reports Change

A customer may lose confidence before the account shows risk. A prospect may decide the brand is unclear before pipeline performance explains the problem. An employee may know a process is creating customer effort long before leadership classifies it as a structural issue.

Static measurement often arrives after the person has already done the emotional work. They have already compared, searched, and decided how much energy the relationship deserves. A quarterly score can tell the company where it arrived. It rarely tells the company how belief moved on the way there.

The customer relationship is alive, but many business systems are designed to take snapshots. A snapshot can be accurate and still incomplete. It can show the position without showing the direction. It can show the outcome without showing the sequence. It can show the average without showing the group whose belief is changing fastest.

A customer experiences the moment, the memory, the effort, and the proof available to them when they are deciding what to do next, not the average. Sequence is what turns scattered evidence into meaning. A phrase appears, a question repeats, a competitor begins to show up in AI answers: each piece matters more when leaders can see the order in which it happened.

## From Reporting to Interpretation

Reporting asks what happened. Interpretation asks what the movement means. Both are necessary, but they produce different kinds of judgment.

A service dashboard shows that response time improved. Interpretation asks whether customers feel more confident because of it. A product dashboard shows that feature usage increased. Interpretation asks whether usage reflects deeper adoption or value extraction before departure. A financial dashboard shows that renewal stayed steady. Interpretation asks whether trust continuity is strengthening or whether customers are remaining because leaving takes more effort than staying.

Leaders need this distinction because the customer relationship spans populations the dashboard misses. A current customer reveals delivered experience. A lost customer reveals the memory that travels through the market. A competitor's customer reveals where switching may become possible. Each group tells a different part of the story, and flattening them into one satisfaction average loses the part that matters most for the next decision.

## Reading Movement as a Discipline

The discipline begins with a question few dashboards ask: is the same meaning appearing across more than one place, in more than one population, and is it increasing or fading?

Evidence has different weights. A single complaint describes one moment, not the whole relationship. A viral post attracts attention, but attention is different from decision impact. Evidence becomes useful when it reflects a pattern, not just a moment. The discipline is to ask who is speaking, where the language appears, when it began, and what it suggests about what the customer may do next.

The most useful readings come from intersections: moments when separate evidence streams point toward the same meaning. A dashboard says engagement is rising. Customer language shows departure questions increasing. AI answers show the brand being compared unfavorably on the question the prospect is actually asking. No single source would have shown that condition. The intersection does.

Tools like ATLAS³ read these intersections systematically, tracking language, populations, AI answer positions, and friction patterns across time. The discipline is available without the tool: build the habit of reading across sources, separating who is speaking from what they are saying, and watching what repeats before acting on what shouts.

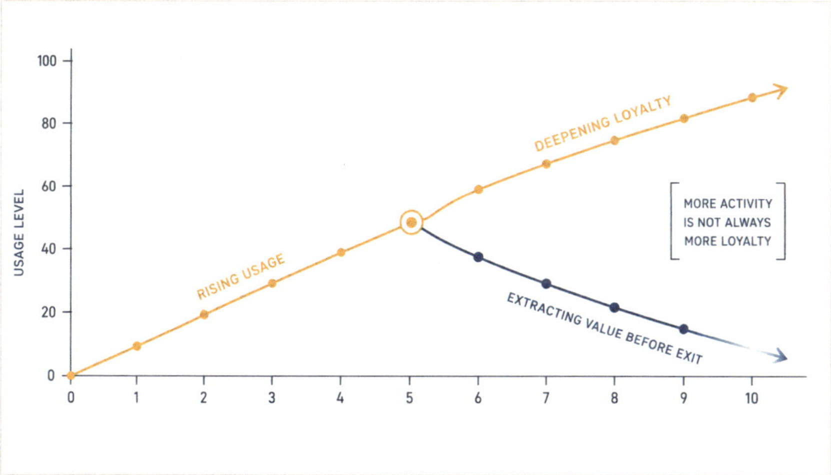


**Figure 8.1** Engagement or extraction.

More activity does not always mean more loyalty. Sometimes it means customers are extracting value before belief turns.

Experience intelligence becomes actionable when leaders connect what the standard reading shows to what the underlying movement may mean.

| Standard reading | What experience intelligence asks | Leadership meaning |
|---|---|---|
| Engagement is rising | Does the activity reflect loyalty or value extraction before departure? | Check trust and future-intent language before treating the metric as good news. |
| Satisfaction is stable | Is belief moving outside the measured sample? | Review departure language, search questions, and reviews beyond the survey population. |
| Brand visibility is improving | Does the visibility create trust, confusion, or comparison? | Inspect whether AI answers mention, compare, prefer, or default to the brand. |
| Complaint volume is flat | Is decision language rising in populations the company does not survey? | Separate burden language from switching language. |
| Operations improved | Is the improvement visible to customers and to AI answer systems? | Turn operational proof into retrievable customer evidence. |
| Adoption is strong | Does use reflect confidence or extraction before exit? | Read usage beside belief language and customer emotion movement. |

A metric can be true and still incomplete. Experience intelligence identifies the meaning underneath the metric. That meaning is what determines the decision.

### Building the Experience Intelligence Review

The review runs beside existing CX reporting. It adds to the dashboard rather than replacing it. It helps the dashboard speak more clearly by asking what the numbers leave out.

It begins with movement, not position. What belief is gaining strength? What belief is weakening? Which customer language is repeating, and in which populations? Which friction is becoming more visible? Which AI answer results are shaping early belief in the market? A strong experience intelligence review raises those questions before the lagging metric confirms what the customer already knew.

The format matters less than the discipline. A thirty-minute conversation, held monthly, that begins with evidence outside the dashboard and asks which condition the organization can improve is more valuable than a quarterly presentation that begins and ends with scores.

Product leaders bring whether adoption reflects confidence. Marketing brings whether reach is creating understanding or comparison. Service brings whether recovery is restoring trust. Finance brings whether value feels fair. Each function contributes a piece of the movement that no single function can see on its own.

---

*The quarterly snapshot will always be taken. Experience intelligence is the discipline of watching what moves between the frames.*

PART THREE

# The Human and Financial Bridge

CHAPTER NINE

# The 3Rs: Reputation, Reach, and Relationships

Some companies are everywhere and trusted by almost nobody. Their name appears across every channel and every comparison table. The awareness metrics look strong. Ask someone who actually uses them how they feel and the language gets careful.

Other companies are trusted deeply by nearly everyone who knows them and found by almost no one who does not. Their customers stay and tell others. Their reach is narrow and their reputation is deep.

Both positions are unsustainable on their own. The first has an attention problem. The second has a discovery problem. Both are symptoms of the same condition: the three forces that build durable market belief are drifting apart.

Those three forces are Reputation, Reach, and Relationships.

Reputation shows whether belief is forming. Reach shows where the experience can be found. Relationships show whether trust becomes continuity. When these three move together, visibility earns consideration and consideration builds belonging. When they separate, leaders mistake attention for trust, distribution for depth, or growth for health.

| The company calls it | The customer experiences it as |
|---|---|
| Reputation | Confidence or caution before the first interaction |
| Reach | Access, relevance, or noise |
| Relationship | Continuity, trust, and belonging |

The 3Rs matter because they connect what the company manages to what the customer actually feels. Keeping those meanings connected is where CX leadership and market strategy meet.

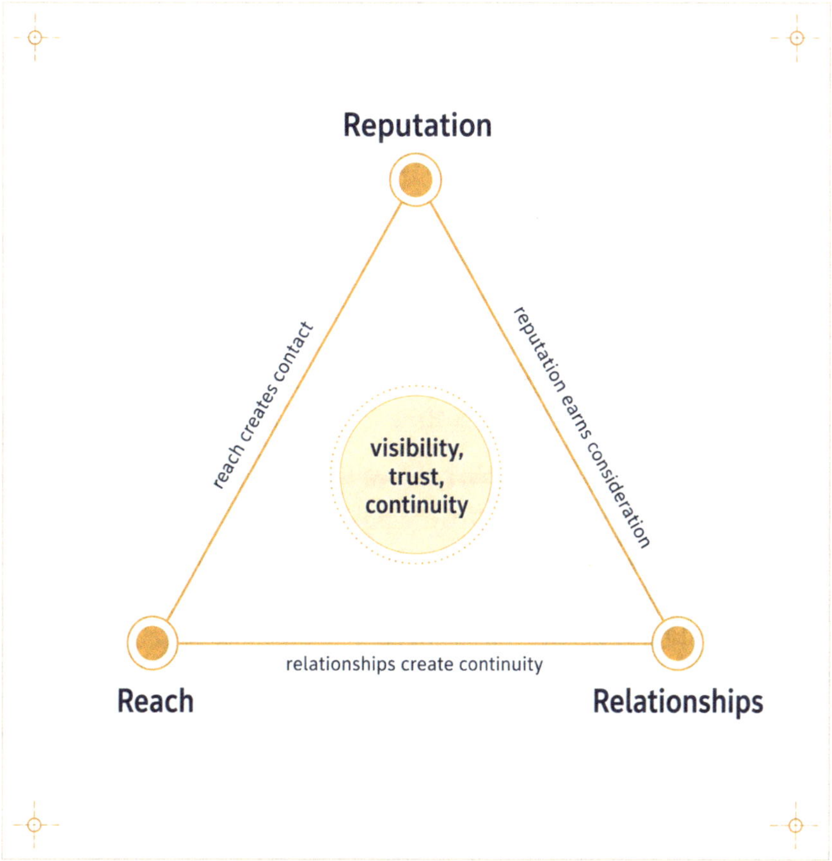


**Figure 9.1** The 3R triangle.

Reach creates contact. Reputation earns consideration. Relationships create continuity.

## Reputation Is Belief Made Visible

Reputation is evidence of belief already forming, not a communications strategy.

A company can declare what it wants to be known for. The market decides what it believes. That belief forms through the match between promise and experience. When the company says one thing and customers consistently experience another, reputation follows the experience. When the company promises clearly and delivers consistently, reputation becomes stronger because belief has proof beneath it.

Reputation is what people believe the company will do when something matters, not what they have heard about the company. Whether it will be honest, easy to deal with, and fair when something goes wrong. A strong reputation reduces uncertainty before the customer has had a direct experience. It gives them a reason to approach.

Reputation grows when the company repeatedly gives people evidence that the promise is true. A product that works as described. A support team that resolves with care. A billing experience that feels fair. The customer experiences those as evidence of what the company is, not as separate departments. Reputation is the market's memory of that evidence.

### Reach Is Access With Meaning

Reach is often treated as audience size. In CX, it means something more specific: whether the right people can find a believable path into the experience.

A company can reach more people without creating more trust. That happens when distribution grows faster than relationship depth. The brand becomes visible to people who do not yet understand it, believe it, or see themselves inside the promise. Reach without belief creates exposure without connection. Reach with reputation creates consideration. Reach with relationships creates belonging.

This distinction matters because organizations frequently confuse expansion with acceptance. They enter new channels or new markets and assume visibility will create growth. Visibility raises the standard as it extends. More people see the promise and test it against the lived experience. More people decide whether the brand has earned the right to speak to them.

The customer wants to be recognized as a person, not targeted as a segment. A community begins to trust when the brand demonstrates that it understands the people it hopes to serve, not just their purchasing behavior. AI answers, search, and social platforms can all extend reach. Each expansion point has to answer the same belief question: what will people believe when they encounter us here?

### Relationships Turn Trust Into Continuity

A relationship is the customer's belief that continuing with the company makes sense, not a transaction repeated many times.

That belief is built through value, consistency, and memory. The customer feels that the company understands enough, helps enough, and respects enough to remain part of their life or work. A relationship strengthens when each interaction respects the last one: the company remembers, the product improves, the service recovers well, and the pricing stays clear. The brand behaves consistently enough for the customer to keep extending belief.

This is different from lock-in. Lock-in depends on difficulty leaving. Trust continuity depends on usefulness staying. Shrink to Human asks leaders to build experiences that remain worth choosing, not to trap customers inside systems.

Relationships also begin inside the company. Employees become loyal to purpose before customers become loyal to a brand. When employees doubt the company has given them the tools, trust, and authority to serve well, the customer eventually feels the difference. Reputation, Reach, and Relationships are CX outcomes shaped by the whole system, not only by marketing.

### Reading Whether the 3Rs Move Together

Each of the four conditions requires a different response. High reach with low reputation means the evidence environment trails the attention. Strong reputation with weak reach means the company is trusted by those who know it and missed by those who would value it. Reach and reputation without relationships means the experience stops short of continuity.

The strongest position is when the three move together: reputation creates belief, reach makes the experience findable, relationships turn trust into continuity. Reading whether those three are moving together or drifting apart requires looking at evidence the dashboard misses.

Reviews show whether reputation is supported by lived experience or running ahead of it. Search questions show whether reach is creating clarity or confusion. AI answer results show whether the brand is being discovered in a position of strength or comparison. Employee escalation patterns show whether the internal system can support the external promise that reach is creating.

Tools like ATLAS$^3$ read the three together across evidence sources simultaneously. The discipline is available to any organization willing to look: not at each R independently, but at how they are moving relative to each other. A brand that is growing its reach faster than its reputation is accumulating a debt that customer evidence will eventually collect.

The 3Rs become actionable when leaders connect each dimension to the evidence that reveals its health and the response it requires.

| Dimension | What it shows | Evidence to read | If weak, the response is |
|---|---|---|---|
| Reputation | Whether belief is forming | Reviews, AI answer results, repeated customer language | Strengthen the proof that the promise is true. |
| Reach | Where the experience can be found | Search questions, discovery paths, audience access | Make the experience easier to find, understand, and enter. |
| Relationships | Whether trust becomes continuity | Renewal behavior, advocacy, employee confidence | Build usefulness, memory, and belonging before expanding reach. |

## Growing Through the 3Rs

Before expanding reach, leaders should ask whether reputation and relationships are strong enough to support it. That is the discipline the 3Rs create: a check on the sequencing of growth.

If reach is growing faster than reputation, the priority is proof: make the experience strong enough that the evidence environment supports what the attention is promising. If reputation is strong but reach is weak, the priority is findability: ensure the people who would value the brand can find a clear path into the experience. If relationships are thin, the priority is continuity: build the conditions that make staying feel natural before asking for more of the market's attention.

The 3R review belongs inside major CX, marketing, product, and market expansion decisions. It should be brief. Are the three dimensions moving together or drifting apart? The answer to that question changes what needs to happen next.

---

*The market is a set of people deciding whether the company deserves belief, not an audience to capture. The 3Rs give leaders a way to read that decision in progress.*

CHAPTER TEN

# The 4Es: Economic, Efficient, Emotional, and Empathetic

I have sat across from leadership teams that celebrated a fourteen-point improvement in satisfaction scores and a twelve-percent reduction in the cost to serve. Both numbers were real. Neither asked what the improvement had cost the customers who produced it, or what the cost reduction had transferred onto the employees who absorbed it.

The 4Es are a discipline for asking those questions.

Economic. Efficient. Emotional. Empathetic. These four dimensions connect what most organizations evaluate separately. Leaders discuss cost, efficiency, retention, and revenue in one room. They discuss trust, empathy, confidence, and belonging in another. Customers experience all four together.

A company can reduce cost and still increase customer effort. It can automate a process and still make the customer feel alone. It can improve the score without improving the relationship. The 4Es exist to surface those contradictions before they calcify into strategy.

When a CX initiative works across all four dimensions, it creates value that lasts. When it works only on the dimensions easiest to measure, it may look strong in the short term while weakening the trust that continuity depends on.

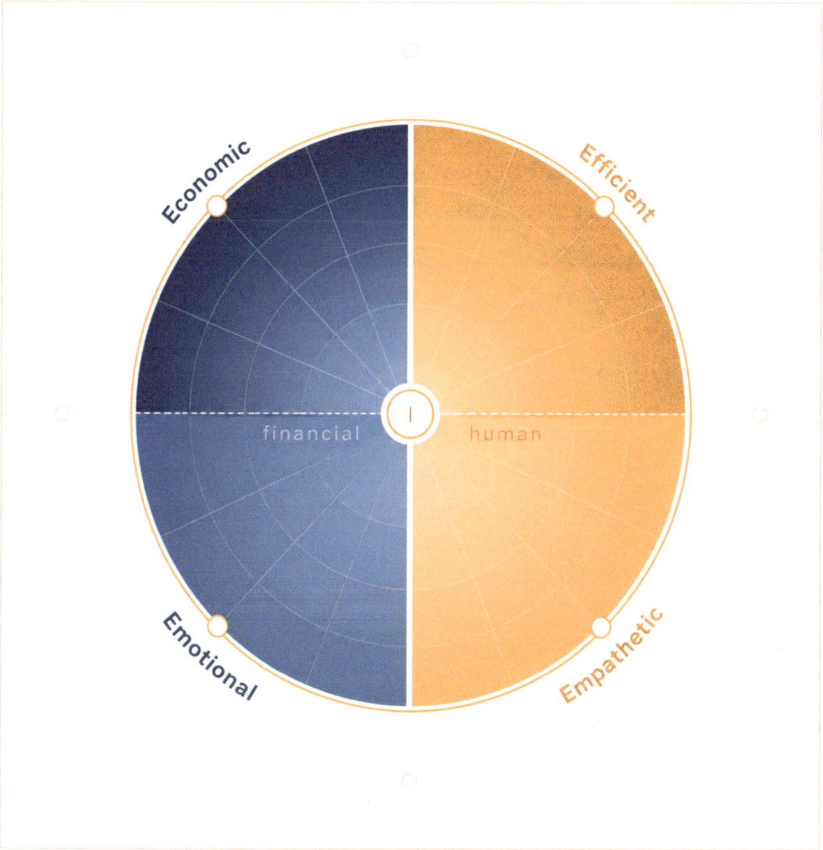


**Figure 10.1** The 4E balance wheel.

The strongest CX decisions work financially because they work humanly.

### Economic Value Is More Than Company Revenue

Economic CX begins with value for the customer, not only for the company.

A customer invests time, attention, and money into a relationship. The company must return something that feels worth that investment. The return may be speed, reduced risk, or confidence in a better outcome. When the customer can feel that return, economic value becomes part of the experience.

Customers judge value by what the relationship helps them accomplish, not by price alone. A more expensive service can feel fair when it saves effort and produces a better outcome. A cheaper service can feel costly when it creates confusion, delay, and doubt. Economic value is the customer's belief that the exchange makes sense.

That belief has direct financial consequences: it influences renewal, retention, and advocacy. Customers who can feel and explain the value they are receiving are easier to retain and more likely to extend the relationship. The economic dimension keeps CX connected to business performance, and it keeps business performance connected to customer reality.

The question this dimension asks: does the experience help the customer feel that the relationship is worth continuing?

### Efficiency Should Reduce Effort, Not Human Judgment

Customers value experiences that are easier, faster, and less repetitive. Efficiency is a genuine gift when it gives the customer time and confidence back. The problem begins when it is treated as the whole experience.

A process can be faster and still feel worse. A chatbot can deflect volume and leave customers unsupported. A shorter interaction can improve a dashboard metric while leaving the customer less confident than before. These are failures of scope rather than failures of efficiency: the efficiency was measured against the company's cost, not against the customer's experience.

True efficiency reduces unnecessary effort without stripping away human judgment. The test is whether the person became more confident with less effort, not whether the process became faster.

Efficiency becomes a problem when it transfers work from the company to the customer. The customer has to search for information the company should have made clear. They have to re-explain what was said in the previous interaction. They have to work around a system that was designed to protect the company's cost rather than honor their time. When that happens, efficiency has improved the report without improving the experience.

The question this dimension asks: did this change reduce effort for the customer and the employee, or did it move the burden somewhere less visible?

### Emotion Shows What the Experience Makes People Believe

Emotion is the felt evidence of belief, not decoration.

A customer feels relief when the system helps. They feel confidence when the next step is clear. They feel doubt when the explanation differs from the experience. These emotional states are part of business outcomes. They influence patience, advocacy, and whether the customer gives the company room to recover when something goes wrong.

A customer emotion score is more useful than a generic satisfaction score when it is tied to the brand's actual promise. Every brand requires a different emotional state from the people who use it. A generic score flattens that difference. A customer emotion score makes the goal legible to every person who shapes the experience.

The question this dimension asks: what does this experience make the customer believe about us? That question moves emotion from a soft consideration into a strategic one.

## Empathy Recognizes the Person Around the Transaction

Empathy is an operating condition for retention and loyalty, not a personality trait.

A customer contacting support may need more than an answer. They may need to stop wasting time, to feel believed, or to find a path forward that respects the pressure they are under. A customer dealing with a billing error may be protecting a relationship with their own customer on the other end. Empathy means the company can see the life around the transaction, not only the transaction itself.

Empathy also applies to employees. A frontline worker who wants to help but lacks authority is in an empathy failure condition. A manager supervising too many people to coach any of them well is in an empathy failure condition. The customer eventually feels both. Empathy sees the person inside the system on both sides of the experience.

Empathy works within standards, not by removing them or saying yes to every request. It gives judgment better context. It changes how leaders design service, automation, escalation, policy, and recovery.

The question this dimension asks: what pressure is this person experiencing, and how can the system help them move forward with dignity?

### Reading 4E Balance

Customer language is the most direct signal of which dimension is under pressure. When customers ask whether something is worth it, the Economic dimension needs attention. When they say a process takes too long, the Efficient dimension does. When they say they have lost trust in the company, the Emotional dimension does. When they say the company misunderstands their situation, the Empathetic dimension does.

Employees reveal the same imbalances before customers do. When employees say the process is too hard to follow, Efficiency needs attention. When they say they lack the power to solve the issue customers keep raising, Empathy needs attention: the system is asking them to absorb emotional labor without the authority to address the cause.

Tools like ATLAS[3] connect customer language, review patterns, search questions, AI answer results, and employee escalation patterns to identify which dimension is creating the strain. The discipline is available without the tool: build the habit of reading customer and employee language through all four dimensions before concluding that a metric result tells the full story.

The 4Es help leaders interpret what kind of improvement is needed. Each dimension requires a different response. Clarifying value addresses the Economic dimension. Reducing friction addresses the Efficient one. Restoring confidence addresses the Emotional one. Redesigning the experience around the person's context addresses the Empathetic one. Without that separation, organizations improve one dimension while weakening another.

The 4Es become actionable when leaders apply them as a review discipline before and after major decisions.

| Dimension | What it protects | The question it asks |
|---|---|---|
| Economic | Durable value for the customer and organization | Does the customer feel the relationship is worth continuing? |
| Efficient | Time, clarity, and reduced unnecessary effort | Did we make the experience easier without moving the burden elsewhere? |
| Emotional | Trust, confidence, and continuity | What belief state does this experience create? |
| Empathetic | Context, pressure, dignity, and forward movement | Does the system recognize the person around the transaction? |

Before a rollout, the table reveals whether the design is balanced. After a rollout, it reveals whether the change worked in both human and financial terms. An initiative that looks economically strong because it lowers cost may reveal on 4E review that customer effort increased. An initiative that looks efficient because it reduces contact volume may reveal that customers now feel alone.

The table helps the business move with better judgment rather than slowing it down.

## The 4E Decision Review

Any meaningful CX initiative should move through all four dimensions before it is approved, scaled, or celebrated. The review asks whether the initiative creates durable value the customer can feel, whether it reduces effort while protecting the customer and the employee, whether it creates the belief state the brand's promise requires, and whether it recognizes the person's context and dignity.

The review belongs across every function. Product teams evaluate whether features create confidence or confusion. Service teams evaluate whether recovery restores dignity or just closes the ticket. Finance leaders evaluate whether pricing creates fairness or doubt. Technology leaders evaluate whether tools make judgment easier or harder for the people who use them.

When all four work together, Customer Experience stops being a cost center or a service program. It becomes a disciplined way to create value that people can feel and the business can sustain.

Economic keeps the business honest. Efficient keeps the system usable. Emotional keeps belief visible. Empathetic keeps the person present.

---

*Those four questions, asked together before a decision is made, change what the decision looks like when it comes back.*

CHAPTER ELEVEN

# Employee Experience Is Where CX Becomes Human First

In contact centers on three continents I have watched a version of the same moment play out. An agent has the answer in forty seconds. She cannot apply it. The policy requires escalation. The queue is long. She explains the situation to the customer three times while they wait. She apologizes for things she did not do.

The customer gives the interaction a low score. The agent is flagged for a long handle time.

Both outcomes miss what happened. The system failed both of them in the same moment.

Employee experience and customer experience are two sides of the same system condition, not two separate programs. Before the customer feels the brand, an employee feels the system. When the employee is blocked from acting, the customer goes without help. When the employee is constrained, the customer feels the constraint.

A customer rarely sees the escalation rule or the supervisor span. They feel the effects. They feel it when the employee is kind but lacks the authority to resolve. They feel it when the employee places them on hold to search for an answer the system should have made clear. They feel it when the script misses the moment.

Employee experience is where CX becomes human first, not a support topic.

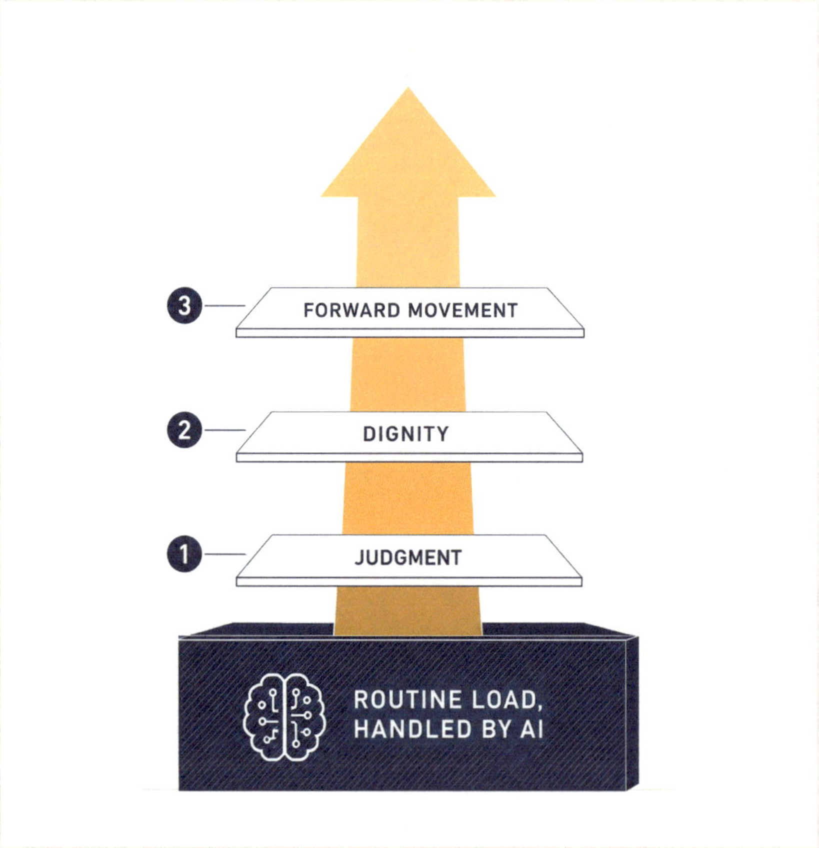


**Figure 11.1** The dignity upgrade.

AI creates value when it raises human judgment, dignity, and forward movement.

## The Human Problem Inside the Employee System

Most people start work wanting to be good at what they do. They want to be useful, respected, and given feedback that helps them improve. Those needs remain. The systems around them have changed dramatically.

Work is now distributed across remote teams, global operations, and systems built without the goal of making the work simpler. A frontline employee may support customers they never see, through systems built by teams they never meet, under rules they did not design, with tools that often miss the emotional reality of the conversation.

A supervisor may be responsible for twenty-five to thirty remote agents. They may rarely see those agents face to face. They are expected to coach, monitor quality, protect morale, and handle escalation across a span that makes meaningful attention difficult. Without the right tools, that span creates distance. The manager sees too little. The employee receives too little. The customer eventually feels the result.

The same pattern appears across every customer-facing function. A product manager may miss the words customers use when the experience becomes confusing. A store manager may know which policy creates customer tension but lack authority to change it. A customer success manager may understand adoption risk before the dashboard shows account decline. Employees often know where the experience strains first. Strong CX leadership treats that knowledge as evidence.

Employee experience covers more than engagement. It is about whether the organization has built the conditions for employees to use judgment, strengthen trust, and help customers move forward.

## Employee Dignity Creates Customer Confidence

Dignity is visible in the work, not an abstract idea in CX.

An employee has dignity when they understand what they are trying to create, have access to what they need to create it, and are trusted with enough authority to act when something goes wrong. The customer feels that dignity as confidence. A supported employee can listen more carefully, explain more clearly, and use judgment instead of hiding behind process.

This matters most in contact centers and frontline service environments, where many workers come from communities that have had limited access to strong paths to professional growth. For those employees, good CX work can become more than service delivery. It can become skill development, economic mobility, and a step toward a stronger future. That is why the employee experience argument is also a dignity argument.

If the company wants employees to deliver trust, it must give them a system they can trust. If the company wants employees to create confidence, it must give them confidence in the tools, policies, and leadership around them. If the company wants employees to show empathy, it must design a work environment where empathy is possible.

A person who is rushed, unsupported, and denied authority will struggle to create a human experience for the customer. A person who receives clarity, support, and room to grow can bring real judgment to the work. Personal growth and corporate growth are the same condition, not forces in tension.

### AI and the Dignity Upgrade

AI has the potential to improve employee experience when it removes burden and raises human judgment. That is the test.

In many service environments, frontline work has required employees to repeat the same answers, search the same knowledge bases, and absorb the same emotional pressure, interaction after interaction. When AI handles routine classification, knowledge retrieval, and repetitive triage, human employees can move toward work that requires judgment. They can evaluate the quality of AI outputs, identify where automation misses the customer's reality, and become architects of the knowledge the system depends on.

That is a different future for frontline work. The agent stops being a throughput processor. The agent becomes part of the intelligence loop: helping the model understand what customers actually mean, reviewing whether AI answers are accurate and fair, feeding lived customer evidence back into the system.

The risk is using AI only to deflect cost. When AI is aimed only at reducing contact volume, it creates distance between the company and the customer. When AI is designed to support employees and improve their judgment, it creates a stronger experience for both sides.

The question is what the employee can do better because of it, not only what AI can do.

Employee conditions translate directly into customer experience conditions. The connection between them is what most CX operating reviews miss.

| Employee condition | Customer effect | Leadership response |
| --- | --- | --- |
| Clear expectations | Customers receive more consistent guidance | Define what good experience looks like in daily work. |
| Honest feedback | Employees improve before habits harden | Give managers time and tools for useful coaching. |
| Better knowledge access | Customers spend less effort repeating and waiting | Make answers easy to find and keep them current. |
| Appropriate authority | Recovery feels more human and complete | Give frontline teams decision rights for common issues. |
| Manageable supervisor span | Employees feel seen and supported | Reduce distance between managers and remote teams. |
| AI-supported routine work | Employees can focus on judgment and quality | Redirect saved capacity into coaching and improvement. |

The goal is to recognize that employee conditions are customer conditions, not to add another people program beside CX. The customer feels what the employee can support.

### Putting Employee Conditions Inside the CX Review

Most organizations review customer outcomes and employee outcomes in separate reports. CX covers satisfaction, effort, and service performance. HR covers engagement, turnover, and workforce capacity. The customer experiences the connection between those two reports every time they contact the company.

A modern CX review should ask where employee conditions are shaping customer belief. It should look at supervisor span, coaching frequency, knowledge access, escalation limits, and the authority employees have to resolve common issues. These are experience conditions, not internal management concerns.

The review should ask how AI is changing the work. Is it removing unnecessary burden or adding oversight complexity? Is it improving employee judgment or narrowing the employee's role? Is it helping managers coach or giving them more dashboards without more time?

The agent had the answer. The system would not let her use it. That is a design problem, not a service quality problem. Design problems are fixed by the functions that created them, not by the people who are asked to work around them.

---

*CX starts with the customer. But it is built by the employee. Every system that ignores that sequence will eventually see it in the numbers.*

CHAPTER TWELVE

# Technology Must Make the Manager's Job Simpler

The question I ask before endorsing any CX technology deployment is whether the manager's job will be simpler on the other side of the rollout, not what the technology can do.

That question comes from watching what happens when organizations skip it, not from skepticism about technology. The same tool that clarifies work in one environment spreads confusion faster in another. Technology amplifies the system it enters. If the system is clear, the tool makes it clearer. If the system is confused, the tool accelerates the confusion. What stays the same is the technology. What changes is what the technology finds when it arrives.

The manager is the point where technology either becomes real or remains a system announcement. If a deployment adds complexity to the manager's day without giving them clearer judgment or better coaching ability, adoption becomes fragile. The tool exists in theory. In practice, people find workarounds, ignore outputs, or wait for the system to be replaced by the next one.

Technology earns its place when it makes the work simpler, clearer, and more human for the people who do it.

### The Human Problem Behind Technology Adoption

People accept useful tools. They resist tools that make their work harder while pretending to make the company smarter.

A frontline manager already stands between leadership, employees, and customers. Leadership wants better performance and cleaner reporting. Employees want useful coaching and room to do good work. Customers want answers and fairness. The manager handles all three expectations simultaneously.

When new technology enters that environment, it has to reduce pressure somewhere real. It should help the manager understand the team faster, reveal where employees need support, and make customer evidence easier to interpret. When it does those things, it strengthens CX. When it adds dashboards without adding clarity, it becomes part of the burden it was supposed to remove.

A new tool can show more data while giving the manager less time to coach. Automation can reduce contact volume while increasing customer frustration somewhere else. A knowledge system can exist and fail if the answers are stale or disconnected from what the customer actually asked. The customer eventually feels all of it. They feel it when the employee navigates too many systems to find a simple answer. They feel it when speed is being measured while judgment is what the moment requires.

Technology adoption is a human experience issue, not an IT issue.

### Technology as an Experience Amplifier

The clearest way to evaluate a CX technology is to ask what it does to the conditions it enters, not what it does in isolation.

A chatbot improves experience when it gives customers fast answers and frees employees for more complex situations. The same chatbot weakens experience when it blocks access to human help and forces customers to repeat themselves. A knowledge assistant improves experience when it gives employees accurate answers in the flow of work. The same assistant weakens experience when it produces generic responses that miss the customer's situation. A performance dashboard improves experience when it helps managers coach in time. The same dashboard weakens experience when it becomes surveillance without support.

The pattern is consistent. Technology strengthens CX when it improves human judgment, reduces unnecessary effort, and helps people act with more confidence. Three things need to improve together: the customer should experience less effort and stronger confidence; the employee should experience clearer expectations and better information; the manager should experience better visibility and a more useful coaching rhythm. When only one improves, leaders need to ask where the burden moved.

**Figure 12.1** One tool, three gains at once.

Technology creates CX value when it strengthens manager clarity, employee judgment, and customer confidence at the same time.

### Reading Whether Technology Is Improving Experience or Moving Effort

Technology outcomes need interpretation because a metric improvement can occur without an experience improvement.

Support volume declines after automation. The metric looks good. Customer language may show frustration rather than relief. Response time improves. Customers may feel processed rather than helped. Self-service adoption rises. Customers may be choosing self-service because human support has become harder to reach, not because the self-service is genuinely useful.

The same reading applies inside the organization. If employees begin using new language after a rollout, that language matters. They may say the tool helps them coach better. They may say AI saves time but produces answers they cannot trust. They may say customers arrive more frustrated because automation failed before the human conversation began. A technology succeeds when it improves the work people actually do and strengthens the belief customers actually form, not because it launched.

Tools like ATLAS[3] read these patterns across customer language, employee escalation patterns, review content, and AI answer results. The discipline is available through structured listening: track what employees say about the tool in the weeks after deployment, watch whether customer language around the affected journey improves or deteriorates, and treat both as equal signals of whether the technology is doing what it was designed to do.

Technology becomes easier to judge when leaders connect each tool to the human condition it is designed to improve.

| Technology use | Human condition it should improve | The question to ask |
|---|---|---|
| AI chat or virtual assistant | Customer clarity and faster resolution | Does it solve the issue or move effort to the customer? |
| Knowledge assistant | Employee confidence and answer quality | Can employees find and trust the answer in the flow of work? |
| Performance dashboard | Manager coaching and timely support | Does it help managers improve people, or only monitor them? |
| AI interaction summary | Context continuity across channels | Does the customer avoid repeating the same story? |
| Workflow automation | Reduced manual burden | Does it free employees for higher judgment work? |
| Quality monitoring | Better coaching and fair evaluation | Does it create useful feedback employees can act on? |

If a tool improves a metric but increases burden for customers, employees, or managers, the design needs more work. If it creates better human judgment, clearer action, and stronger trust, it deserves to scale. The goal is better experience through better work, not technology adoption.

### The Manager Adoption Test

Before a tool is approved, scaled, or celebrated, ask whether it makes the manager's job simpler. Not whether it removes all complexity: serious work requires judgment. Whether it makes the work clearer, more visible, more coachable, and more useful.

If the tool helps only the company report more, it is incomplete. If it helps the customer but creates unmanageable employee strain, it is incomplete. If it helps employees but leaves customers more confused than before, it is incomplete.

Run a technology impact review after every major CX deployment. Look at customer language, employee language, and manager workload. Ask what the tool made easier, what it made harder, who absorbed the new burden, and what human judgment became possible because the tool exists. This review should happen early enough to improve the rollout, not after frustration has hardened into habit.

The strongest organizations treat technology as part of the human system, not as a replacement for it. They ask whether tools lift human judgment or erase it. They protect clarity, coaching, and authority as CX assets rather than variables to optimize away.

---

*Technology that earns its place makes the manager's job simpler, the employee's work clearer, and the customer's experience easier to trust. That is the test. Everything else is a feature.*

PART FOUR

# Leadership, Governance, and Accountability

CHAPTER THIRTEEN

# Leadership Belief Before Titles

A title can assign ownership. It cannot create belief.

I have met Chief Customer Officers who could not get a return call from the product team. I have met CX directors whose recommendations were reviewed quarterly, absorbed into existing programs, and quietly neutralized. The title gave the work a home, not traction.

The organization's behavior changes when people believe the customer relationship belongs to them: when the product manager asks the belief question before shipping a feature, when the finance leader considers the trust cost of a pricing decision, when the middle manager treats customer language as evidence rather than complaint. Those changes happen when belief is present. They follow belief, not titles.

Leadership begins when enough people in the organization believe the customer relationship belongs to them. A strong leader can start that belief moving. A title can support it. Governance can reinforce it. Accountability can measure it. Belief itself remains irreplaceable.

A CX leader without organizational belief becomes a symbol. A CX leader with organizational belief becomes a force multiplier. The difference is visible in how the work moves. When belief is weak, CX depends on persuasion and repeated explanation. When belief is strong, teams begin asking customer questions inside their own work before the CX leader has to ask.

The strongest CX leaders help the organization believe it already owns part of the customer relationship rather than trying to own the whole thing themselves.

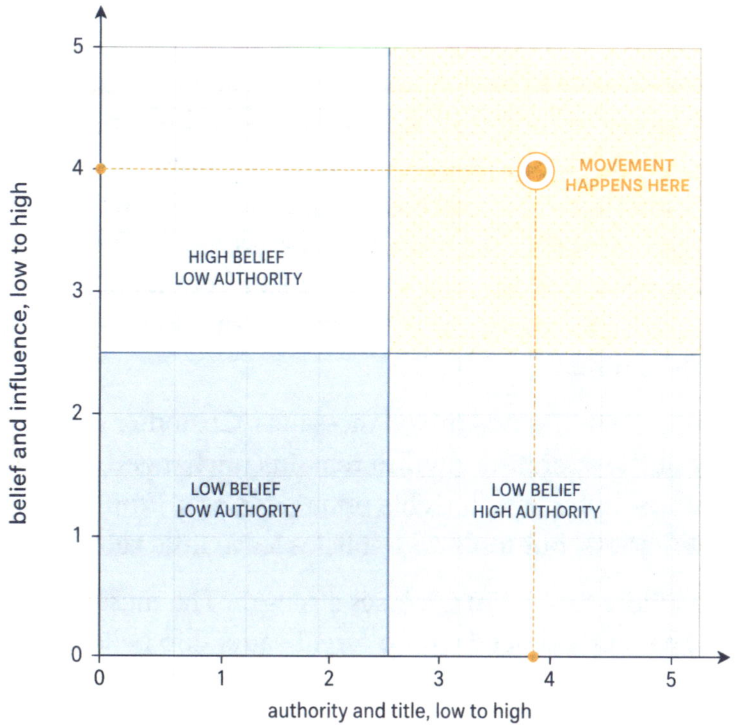


**Figure 13.1** Title and belief.

Belief plus influence creates movement, not the title alone.

## The Human Problem Inside Top-Down Change

People inside organizations have learned to protect themselves from temporary initiatives.

They have seen new priorities arrive with strong language and weak follow-through. They have seen leadership teams ask for customer focus while continuing to reward speed, volume, and departmental targets. They have seen new dashboards added without old burdens removed. When CX arrives as another top-down mandate, people listen carefully and ask whether it will still be the priority in six months.

This is resistance to incoherence, not resistance to the customer. Most employees want to do good work. The problem begins when the structure asks people to believe one thing while rewarding another. A service leader asked to improve trust while being judged on speed. A product leader asked to reduce friction while being rewarded for release volume. A frontline manager asked to coach for experience while supervising too many people with too little time.

The organization sends mixed messages. Customer experience matters, but the operating rhythm remains unchanged. Customer belief matters, but decision rights remain narrow. Employee judgment matters, but tools and policies leave little room to act.

This is where top-down CX loses strength. The message may be right. The method needs more care. Leadership belief means people can see that the organization is willing to improve the conditions that shape the customer's belief. CX is more than an announcement from above. It is made practical in the middle and usable in the field.

### The Leader Who Moves the Matrix

CX needs a leader who can move work across the organization: someone who gives the work enough direction, credibility, and energy to spread.

Committees can coordinate. They rarely move belief. A committee can review metrics and agree on language, but when no one brings conviction the work becomes procedural. People attend, update the slide, and return to the same operating habits. One influential leader changes that. They create a center of gravity that makes the work easier to understand, protects the purpose from dilution, and connects CX to the business without reducing it to a metric.

That leader may have a CX title or an operating one. The title matters less than the ability to move across the system. A strong product leader often has a natural advantage: they already work near the center of use, adoption, and friction. They understand that the promise has to become usable. When they add belief discipline, they can become powerful CX leaders because they already live in the matrix. The same is true of any leader who can move across silos with trust and enough humility to listen to the field.

This is leadership that moves the work, rather than heroic leadership. The leader helps the company become more capable of delivering the customer experience, not becoming it.

### The 20% and the 80%

The CX expert is essential. The CX expert is one part of the force.

The expert brings the diagnostic toolkit: the language, methods, evidence discipline, and frameworks that help the organization see what it has been missing. They can read customer evidence, identify friction, interpret belief movement, and build tools that help others act.

The operating leader shapes the larger share of implementation. They own the daily reality where customer experience becomes real or fades: the people, the rhythms, the tradeoffs, the handoffs. They know which policies are hard to execute, which tools slow teams down, and which changes will work in the field versus which will stay inside a presentation.

The CX expert may be 20% of the force. The operating leader runs the other 80%. That ratio is a reminder that CX must become less dependent on the expert over time, not mathematical precision. If the expert must be present for the experience to work, the system still depends on the expert.

That transfer requires co-creation. The expert brings the outside-in discipline. The operator brings the inside reality. The field tests whether the model can live in daily work. When those three connect, CX gains traction that no single title could have produced.

### The Middle Manager Layer

Middle managers are the most critical layer in CX implementation. They are also the most frequently overlooked.

They receive strategy from above and pressure from below. They translate executive language into coaching, staffing, escalation, and daily behavior. They know when a new initiative will create real improvement and when it will create more work without better outcomes. If they distrust the CX work, implementation slows. If they believe it will help their teams, it gains strength.

They know which systems create repeated customer effort, where scripts fail the conversation, and which tools help versus which add burden. A smart CX leader treats that knowledge as evidence, not as reluctance to manage.

Middle managers are interpreters of reality, not blockers by nature. When they are included early in the design, they protect the work from becoming abstract. When they are informed only at rollout, they protect their teams by minimizing the change. The difference between those two outcomes is when the conversation starts.

Leadership belief becomes practical when each layer understands what it must support and what strengthens the work.

| Leadership layer | What it must support | What strengthens CX |
|---|---|---|
| Executive sponsor | Direction, priority, and protection | Makes customer belief part of the business rhythm. |
| CX expert | Method, evidence, interpretation, and tools | Helps the organization see and diagnose the experience. |
| Operating leader | Daily execution and tradeoff management | Turns CX into the way work gets done. |
| Middle manager | Translation, coaching, and field adoption | Makes the work usable for teams. |
| Frontline leader | Customer reality and employee confidence | Shows where the system becomes human. |

Each layer supports a different part of the work. When they connect, CX becomes a shared operating discipline rather than a function that reports upward and hopes for agreement.

### From Title to Movement

Before creating another committee, dashboard, or executive role, leaders should ask whether the organization has the belief required to make CX real. Who can move the work across functions? Which operating leader can run the 80%? Which middle managers must trust the work before the field will adopt it?

A CX belief map helps answer those questions. It names the executive sponsor, the CX expert, the operating leader, the middle manager layer, and the frontline evidence sources. It shows how the work moves from direction to method to execution to coaching to customer reality. It also identifies where belief is strong and where it must be earned.

If middle managers see CX as more reporting, belief must be earned there first. If product leaders see CX as a service problem, belief must be earned there. If frontline teams see CX as a slogan, belief must be earned there. The organization should treat those conditions as design requirements, not communication problems.

Leadership belief grows when people can see how the work helps them serve the customer better, operate with more clarity, and create value the business can sustain.

---

*A title can name the work. Belief moves the work.*

CHAPTER FOURTEEN

# Belief Becomes Repeatable Through Systems

There is a useful comparison between a CX expert and a doctor. A doctor can diagnose the condition and describe the treatment. The patient has to live differently after the appointment: different habits, different choices, different daily behavior. The expertise transfers only when the patient acts on it.

CX improvement works the same way. The expert can read the evidence, identify the friction, and design the solution. The operating leader has to live differently afterward: different questions in the product review, different evidence in the service meeting, different coaching conversations with frontline managers. That change has to happen inside the daily rhythm of the business, not inside the next workshop.

Belief becomes repeatable when the system can sustain it without the expert in the room.

Repeatability is different from giving every customer the same scripted experience. It means the company has built the conditions that allow the right belief to be created consistently.

People may need different answers, different recovery paths, or different forms of reassurance. The system still needs a shared standard for what confidence, fairness, and dignity should feel like. When belief appears in a regional operator's decision, a product team's tradeoff call, and a service manager's coaching conversation, the system has taken root.

If the experience depends on one expert, one champion, or one moment of executive attention, the system is still fragile.

## The Human Problem Behind Fragile CX

People can support an idea and still struggle to practice it. This is common in Customer Experience. Leaders agree that trust matters. Teams agree the experience should be more human. Employees agree the friction should be reduced. The problem is transfer more often than conviction.

A team leaves a CX session inspired, then returns to old systems. The dashboard still rewards the same behavior. The policy still limits judgment. The manager still lacks time to coach. The belief was real. The system needed more before it could support it.

Employees feel this tension first. They hear leaders speak about trust while their own work conditions create effort. They hear leaders speak about empathy while policies leave little room for judgment. They hear leaders speak about customer obsession while their managers are judged by numbers that miss the full relationship.

Customers feel the tension next. They feel it when the company sounds human in a campaign but rigid in recovery. They feel it when service employees are kind but powerless. They feel it when regional teams interpret the same situation differently.

The issue is often a lack of system rather than a lack of care. A system makes the belief usable. It turns intention into standards, standards into routines, routines into decisions, and decisions into customer confidence.

### From Project to Operating Rhythm

Customer Experience gains strength when it becomes part of how work gets done, not a project alongside it.

A project has a beginning and an end. An operating rhythm repeats. A project depends on attention. A rhythm builds habit. Many CX efforts begin as projects because the organization needs focus. That is useful. The risk comes when the project ends before the operating rhythm begins.

The organization may have clearer language, better workshop output, and new metrics, but the work stays outside the calendar, the coaching model, and the decision rights. The system then returns to what it already knows. Governance prevents that drift.

Governance is more than bureaucracy when it helps people make better decisions. It is the structure that keeps belief visible after the energy of launch fades. It answers the practical questions: who owns which customer condition, which evidence enters the operating rhythm, which standards must work across geographies, and what proof will show whether the change worked.

The strongest CX systems work without constant escalation to the center. They give the field enough clarity to act and enough structure to stay coherent. CX lives where work is planned, built, delivered, and improved, not only in the CX team.

### The Center and the Field

A scaled CX system needs both center and field, and it needs them to build together.

The center protects coherence: the standard, the measurement logic, the evidence discipline, and the shared definition of what good experience means. Without the center, local variation becomes fragmentation. The field protects reality: the market language, the employee constraints, the cultural context, and the moments where the standard must adapt to serve the person well. Without the field, central standards can become elegant and unusable.

The center brings pattern; the field brings context. The center brings standard; the field brings proof. The center brings consistency; the field brings usability. Co-creation is the operating model.

When the center and field build together, standards become stronger because they have been tested by reality. Field teams commit more fully because they can see the purpose behind the standard. A company expanding across countries and cultures cannot depend on individual champions alone. The greeting may change, the language may change, and the channel preference may change. The belief standard should still be clear: customers should feel that the company is reliable, fair, and human wherever the experience appears.

Standardization is different from sameness. It means the operating rhythm can travel.

**Figure 14.1** Center and field.

The center protects coherence. The field protects reality. Co-creation turns both into repeatable experience.

Belief becomes repeatable when leaders know where it should appear in the operating rhythm.

| Rhythm | What it reviews | Why it matters |
|---|---|---|
| Weekly team review | Customer language, employee friction, active recovery issues | Keeps the work close to lived experience. |
| Monthly CX review | Belief movement, customer evidence, AI answer results, operational pressure | Connects customer reality to leadership decisions. |
| Quarterly business review | Trust continuity, retention, adoption, cost-to-serve, standards progress | Connects CX to financial and operating outcomes. |
| Field calibration | Local context, market language, employee constraints, customer proof | Keeps standards useful across geographies. |
| Governance review | Decision rights, accountability, evidence quality, system changes | Keeps the experience from depending on individual champions. |

Each organization will adapt this rhythm to its own size and operating model. The principle stands: belief must have a place to be reviewed, understood, and acted on. If it only appears in a workshop, it fades. If it appears in the operating rhythm at every level, it becomes part of how the company learns.

## Whether Repeatability Is Creating the Right Belief

Repeatability can just as easily preserve weak practice. A company can repeat the wrong thing: standardize friction, scale confusing language, automate a poor recovery path, or make an unfair policy more efficient. The question is whether the process created confidence, not whether teams followed the process.

If customers keep asking the same question, the standard may need to be clearer. If employees keep escalating the same issue, the decision rights may need to be stronger. If AI answer results keep placing the brand in comparison rather than preference, the proof layer may need strengthening.

Tools like ATLAS[3] help leaders track whether belief is moving in the direction the company intends, across populations, channels, and time periods. The discipline is available through any structured listening rhythm: connect the operating review to evidence outside the dashboard, and ask whether the repeated experience is creating the belief customers need in order to continue.

That is the difference between compliance and experience maturity. Compliance asks whether teams followed the process. Experience maturity asks whether the process created confidence.

### Making Belief Repeatable

The practical test is one question: where does customer belief get reviewed inside the business? If the answer is only inside the CX team, the system has more growing to do. Belief must appear in product reviews, finance conversations, operating planning, HR discussions, and regional calibration.

The first step is to identify the operating rhythm and place customer belief inside it. As a standing question in each function's existing review, rather than as a separate agenda item. Product reviews whether use is creating confidence. Finance reviews whether value feels fair. Service reviews whether recovery restores trust.

The second step is to define decision rights. If teams can see the evidence but lack the power to act on it, the rhythm becomes theater. The field needs clarity about what it can adjust, what must be escalated, and what requires cross-functional action.

Middle managers need enough authority to remove friction where it appears.

The third step is to connect local learning to shared standards. When a region solves a customer problem, the organization should learn from it. When a frontline team finds better language, the system should test it. When AI answer results improve because new evidence becomes visible, the organization should understand what changed.

The system learns. The field contributes. The standard improves. The customer experiences more coherence across every market where the brand appears.

---

*A scaled organization earns strength when belief lives across the organization rather than in one person, one team, or one moment of attention.*

CHAPTER FIFTEEN

# Accountability Makes CX Real

I have worked with companies that published CX values on every wall and measured their service teams almost entirely on average handle time. The values said: make the customer feel heard. The metric said: end the call faster. The employees read it clearly. They understood exactly what the company meant.

The customer did too. They felt it as rushed support, incomplete answers, and the persistent sense that the company was managing them toward an exit rather than helping them reach one.

Belief gives CX meaning. Accountability gives it weight.

The deeper test of any CX commitment is what the company measures, reviews, rewards, and protects when decisions become difficult. A customer-centered organization builds trust into operating reviews, connects retention to the functions that shape it, and gives employees the authority required to act. It makes long-term customer value part of leadership accountability, not a separate workstream.

The customer knows what the company values by how the company behaves. Employees know what the company values by how they are measured. Leaders know what the company values by what appears in the conversation when budgets, incentives, and tradeoffs are decided.

Accountability is the bridge between intention and behavior. It is how belief becomes part of the operating system.

**Figure 15.1** The accountability chain.

CX becomes real when board priorities, executive decisions, manager behavior, employee conditions, and customer outcomes are connected.

### The Human Problem Inside Mismatched Measurement

People respond to what the system rewards. That is true for executives, managers, employees, and partners. People may care deeply about the customer, but if the operating system rewards something else, daily behavior will eventually follow the reward.

A service team can be told to protect trust while being measured mostly on speed. A sales team can be told to sell long-term value while being compensated on short-term close. A frontline manager can be told to coach for empathy while supervising too many employees with too little time. The result is mixed instruction, not bad intent.

Employees hear one message in the customer promise and a different message in the performance system. A frontline employee may know the customer needs time, but the metric rewards speed. A product leader may know the experience needs simplification, but the roadmap rewards visible releases. A service leader may know the root cause sits in policy, but the service team is measured on recovery after the policy creates the issue.

Customers feel this contradiction. They feel it as rushed support, incomplete recovery, or promises that differ from delivery. They may not know which internal metric shaped the experience. They only feel the system.

Accountability matters because it connects the system to the promise. It helps employees trust that the organization means what it says about customers. When accountability is clear, people know what customer outcome they are responsible for helping create. That clarity changes behavior.

### Board-Level Attention Changes the Work

Customer Experience gains power when it enters the regular language of governance. The board does not manage daily CX work. But it should understand whether customer belief, trust continuity, and experience quality are supporting the business model.

The board should receive CX as business evidence, not a decorative story: which customer beliefs are strengthening, which friction patterns are increasing cost, and which trust indicators are moving before revenue moves. Those questions help the board see Customer Experience as part of enterprise health rather than a separate department's concern.

This matters because many CX decisions require protection from short-term pressure. The easiest decision may reduce cost this quarter while increasing effort for customers and employees. The fastest automation may reduce contact volume while weakening trust. Board-level attention helps the organization hold a longer view.

Enterprise CX credibility requires top management agreement. A strong standard should inspect more than service behavior. It should inspect whether leadership, governance, measurement, and accountability support the customer outcomes the organization claims to value. The customer experience cannot be certified as an enterprise capability if the leadership model contradicts it.

### Compensation Reveals the Real Priority

People watch what is rewarded. If leaders talk about retention but pay only for acquisition, the organization learns what matters. If leaders talk about trust but reward only speed, employees learn what matters. Compensation is one of the clearest signals inside a company, and it is rarely discussed as a CX issue.

Different roles shape different parts of the customer relationship. Sales should be rewarded for customers who can succeed, not only customers who can be closed. Product should be measured by adoption and customer progress, not only output. Service should be measured by trust restoration and issue prevention, not only contact handling. The goal is to remove the contradiction between what the company says and what it rewards, not to turn every role into a CX role.

If the company wants trust continuity, someone must be accountable for the conditions that create it. If the company wants lower customer effort, someone must be accountable for the friction that produces it. If the company wants employee-powered CX, someone must be accountable for the conditions employees need to deliver. Each of those requires a named owner, a visible metric, and a review that connects the condition to the outcome.

When accountability becomes visible, CX becomes less dependent on persuasion. The system begins to support the work.

### Connecting Accountability to the Right Source

A company can measure the wrong thing with great discipline. It can reward activity that looks productive while belief moves in the wrong direction. It can celebrate lower contact volume while customers are giving up on getting help. It can celebrate engagement while customers are extracting remaining value before leaving.

The stronger accountability model traces the customer condition to the system that created it. Service teams often inherit problems they did not cause. Frontline employees are asked to repair friction that product, policy, billing, or operations produced. A better model identifies the source of the condition and holds that source accountable for improvement, while giving service the fairer role of recovering trust and feeding intelligence back into the organization.

Reading customer language, friction patterns, AI answer results, and employee escalation patterns helps leaders connect the evidence to the function responsible for the condition. If customers repeatedly say support is kind but cannot help, the issue may lie in employee authority or policy design, not in the service team's effort. If prospects ask AI for better alternatives, the issue may lie in proof and positioning, not in marketing spend.

Tools like ATLAS[3] help leaders make those connections systematically. The discipline is available through any structured review: ask not only which team is associated with the complaint, but which condition in the system created it. That question changes where improvement effort is directed.

Accountability becomes more human and more precise when it measures people against the outcomes they can actually shape.

Accountability becomes useful when each function can see the customer outcome it helps create.

| Function | Customer outcome it shapes | Accountability question |
|---|---|---|
| Board and CEO | Enterprise commitment to customer value | Are customer outcomes part of business governance? |
| Product | Adoption, usability, and value realization | Does the product help customers reach value with less effort? |
| Marketing | Expectation, clarity, and belief before purchase | Are we creating demand the experience can honor? |
| Sales | Fit, trust, and healthy customer acquisition | Are we selling customers into success? |
| Service | Recovery, confidence, and issue prevention | Does support restore trust and reduce repeated friction? |
| Finance | Fairness, value clarity, and trust in terms | Do customers believe the exchange is fair? |
| Operations | Reliability and consistency | Does delivery match the promise across time and place? |
| HR | Employee readiness and dignity | Are employees equipped to deliver the experience? |
| Technology | Access, continuity, and better judgment | Do tools make work simpler and customer movement easier? |

This is a starting point for the accountability conversation, not a universal scorecard. Each organization should adapt the outcomes to its own business model and customer promise. The principle stands: when each function can see the belief condition it helps create, CX stops depending on one team to take on the whole relationship.

## The Customer Outcome Accountability Map

Start with the customer belief the company wants to create. Ask which conditions create that belief and which functions shape those conditions. If the desired belief is confidence, map where clarity, reliability, and employee authority are owned. If the desired belief is fairness, map where pricing, policy, and billing decisions are made. If the desired belief is belonging, map where identity, recognition, and continuity are built.

Connect those conditions to operating reviews, metrics, and decision rights. People need to know what customer outcome they are helping create and how their work contributes to it. The map should be reviewed at the executive and board level. It should also be translated into practical expectations for managers and teams.

This is how CX becomes part of business discipline. It is how belief moves from values to governance. It is how the organization stops asking the customer-facing team to absorb conditions the wider system created.

Accountability makes CX real because it gives belief a place in decisions.

---

*When that place is clear, people stop asking whether the customer matters and start asking which customer outcome they are responsible for improving.*

CHAPTER SIXTEEN

# AI Requires Named Human Accountability

Ask someone in your organization who is accountable for what your AI system says to a customer who cannot get help. Ask who is responsible when the model gives a wrong answer at scale. Ask who reviews whether the system treats different customer groups the same way.

Most organizations cannot answer those questions cleanly. They have policies, platform agreements, and vendor contracts. They often lack a person.

Customers experience AI through outcomes. The answer was useful, or it missed the question. The path was clear, or it left them stuck. The escalation worked, or it failed. When those outcomes fall short, customers experience the company, not a technology failure.

Every AI deployment in CX should have a named human owner: someone accountable for what the system is allowed to do, what evidence trains it, and how the organization learns when the model creates confusion, friction, or trust loss. The goal is innovation strong enough to earn trust.

### What Neither Side Can See

Whether an issue came from a model, a workflow, or a platform integration matters little to customers. They experience the company. If the AI answer is wrong, the company is wrong. If the automated path hides the next step, the company is unclear. If the model treats one customer group differently from another, the company's fairness is in question.

Customers often cannot see the system behind the answer. They do not know which data shaped it, whether the model had current information, or whether the company can explain the decision if it is challenged. That uncertainty becomes part of the experience.

Employees face a similar uncertainty. They need to know when to trust the tool, when to override it, and how their own judgment fits into the system. If the model becomes an authority without explanation, employees lose confidence. If AI becomes a support tool with clear boundaries, employees can use it to serve customers better.

The question is whether people can trust how AI is used. Trust requires a person who can answer for the system.

### Transparency Is an Operating Condition

In CX, transparency is both an ethical principle and an operating condition. Customers make better decisions when they understand what kind of interaction they are having. Employees serve better when they understand what the system is recommending and why. Leaders govern better when AI activity is visible enough to review, improve, and correct.

If the customer is interacting with a bot, the company should make that clear. If an AI recommendation influences routing, eligibility, or escalation, the organization should know who owns that logic. If a model is trained on past interactions, leaders should understand that past data reflects the limits and biases of the system that produced it.

The data that trains the model reflects human choices: what was collected, what was excluded, and what the organization historically believed mattered. AI does not remove those choices. It can scale them. That is why named accountability matters. A named owner has to ask whether the model is using current evidence, whether customer groups are treated fairly, and whether the customer has a clear path to a human when the situation requires judgment.

Transparency gives customers clearer expectations, employees clearer authority, and leaders clearer responsibility.

### AI Should Protect the Person While Improving the System

AI can improve the customer relationship when it protects the person and improves the system at the same time. It can help customers find answers faster, reduce repeated explanations, and identify patterns that employees have been noticing quietly. It can help managers coach earlier and reveal friction before it becomes expensive.

A cancellation flow gives a useful test. If AI helps a customer understand options, review consequences, and complete their choice clearly, the system can preserve trust even when the customer leaves. If AI hides the exit, adds confusing steps, or delays the decision to protect short-term revenue, it uses scale against the person who trusted it. The difference is moral and operational. I have seen both in organizations that believed they were doing the right thing.

AI should protect the customer's choice, strengthen the employee's judgment, and give leaders clearer evidence of what the system is actually doing. That is how AI strengthens trust rather than eroding it.

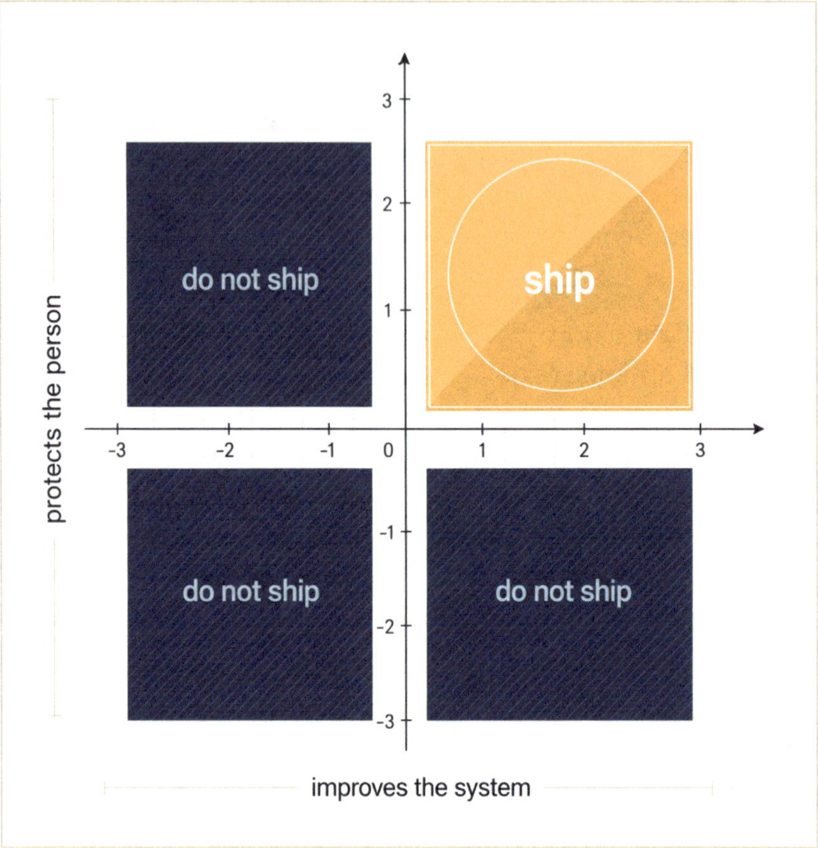


**Figure 16.1** The AI trust test.

The test of AI in CX is whether it protects the person while improving the system.

## When the Metric Moves but Belief Doesn't

AI can change experience in places the company may miss. A chatbot may reduce support volume while customer language shows frustration with access. An AI recommendation may increase conversion while complaints show customers feel misled. An automated summary may save employee time while frontline feedback shows it misses emotional context. Each of these is a signal that the metric improved while the belief condition stayed the same or weakened.

Reading those signals requires connecting technical performance to customer experience evidence. Is the AI improving clarity or creating confusion? Is automation reducing effort or shifting it to the customer? Are employees using the tool with confidence or working around it?

ATLAS³ reads these conditions across customer language, employee escalation patterns, and AI answer positions simultaneously. The discipline is available through any structured review: hold AI deployments to the same evidence standard as any other customer experience decision. Customer language, employee feedback, and trust movement are all part of the governance picture.

AI governance should be reviewed by customer belief, employee judgment, and trust continuity as well as by technical performance. That is the CX leader's role: to ensure every model that touches the customer relationship has a human owner and a customer outcome attached to it, rather than to own every model.

AI accountability becomes practical when each use case has a human owner, a customer condition to protect, and a clear accountability question.

| AI use case | Named human owner | Customer condition to protect | Accountability question |
|---|---|---|---|
| Chat triage | Service leader | Clear path to resolution | Does the customer reach the right help with less effort? |
| Cancellation or renewal | Product or revenue leader | Honest choice and fair treatment | Does the design respect the customer's decision? |
| Agent coaching | Operations leader | Better employee judgment | Does the tool help employees improve with useful feedback? |
| Knowledge assistant | Service or enablement leader | Accurate and current answers | Can employees trust the guidance in the flow of work? |
| AI answer monitoring | CX or marketing leader | Accurate first impression | Does the public proof support how AI explains the brand? |
| Personalization model | Data or experience leader | Relevance without manipulation | Does personalization help the person rather than pressure them? |

Every organization will adapt ownership based on structure, industry, and regulation. The principle stands: AI that shapes the customer relationship needs named human accountability. When ownership is clear, teams can improve the system. When ownership is vague, trust depends on hope.

### Before You Deploy

For every customer-facing or employee-facing AI deployment, build a map that names the owner, the customer condition being protected, and the escalation path. Name the conditions that require human intervention. This needs to become a serious exercise, not a heavy governance one.

I ask three questions about every AI deployment: can the customer reach a human when judgment is needed; does the model treat people fairly across customer groups; and does the design protect trust when the customer chooses to leave. Those three questions cover the conditions where AI most commonly damages belief.

AI standards will differ by country, government, and industry. CX leaders should build responsible habits now rather than waiting for perfect global consensus. The habits companies build now will shape how they use stronger systems later. A company that learns to govern AI with named accountability, human override, and customer dignity will be better prepared as the technology advances.

The current moment is valuable precisely because the technology is still early enough that the habits are still forming.

---

*AI becomes strongest in CX when it helps the company see the person more clearly. Everything else is a capability in search of a purpose.*

PART FIVE

# Standards, Archetypes, and Seeing First

CHAPTER SEVENTEEN

# Standards Turn CX From Outliers Into a Practice

Customer Experience becomes serious when its best work can be taught, repeated, and used across borders.

Every industry has gifted practitioners. Every market has companies that understand the customer better than their peers. Every country has leaders who create trust before anyone has language for what they are doing. That kind of excellence matters. It has limits when it stays trapped inside individual instinct.

A brilliant practitioner can improve one company. A strong operator can improve one region. A gifted service leader can transform one team. But CX needs more than examples. It needs shared language, standards, and pathways that can travel.

Standards help Customer Experience move from scattered excellence to shared professional practice. They strengthen judgment rather than replacing it, and they create common ground without making every company the same. Standards help practitioners understand what good work requires across different markets, cultures, and operating conditions.

A practitioner in São Paulo and a practitioner in Dubai should be able to use the same language. They may serve different markets and work in different languages. They can still share what is meant by trust, fairness, employee enablement, and customer evidence. Standards give CX a common floor. Great practitioners can build above it.

I built the Global CX Alliance because CX needs language, standards, and pathways that can travel. Customer Experience has matured beyond isolated practice. It now needs a professional structure that helps people grow, helps organizations improve, and helps the discipline earn credibility across cultures and markets.

### The Human Need for Shared Meaning

People grow faster when they can see where they are on a path. That is true for customers. It is true for employees. It is true for practitioners.

A CX professional trying to build a career needs more than inspiration. They need language for what they do, proof that the work matters, and a pathway that lets their credibility travel beyond one company or one market. Many CX practitioners built their skill through lived experience: listening to customers, solving problems, and helping organizations see what customers were already trying to say. That experience is valuable. CX becomes stronger when it connects to shared standards.

A practitioner should be able to explain what they know. A hiring leader should be able to understand what a credential means. A company should be able to assess whether its CX maturity is emerging, developing, or advanced. Those things require shared reference points.

Without a shared pathway, practitioners can feel isolated. They may believe in the work but struggle to explain their value. Teams may care about customers but lack common language for improvement. Executives may support CX but lack a disciplined way to judge maturity. Standards create the reference point. They help people feel that the work has shape.

### The Same Questions, Every Market

A standard makes practice portable. That matters in a global economy.

Customer Experience now crosses countries, cultures, and multinational operating models. A company may design in one market, support from another, and rely on customer evidence that moves across all of them. The experience must still make sense to the person receiving it.

Standards help organizations sustain quality across that complexity without forcing every market into identical expression. Global consistency is different from cultural sameness. A greeting may change. A channel preference may change. The pace of trust formation may change. Standards help leaders ask the right questions about fairness, employee confidence, and evidence discipline even when local answers differ.

Government continuity matters here. When governments treat citizens as customers and experiences as policy priorities, they create conditions for stronger service practice. Dubai is a working example: continuity of leadership, ambition at the service level, and citizen experience treated as a policy priority have shaped the private sector culture around it. When public systems take experience seriously, the standard rises for everyone operating inside that market.

Standards help that learning travel beyond individual markets.

### Entry Points at Every Level

CX standards need to serve more than large organizations. CX grows when the pathway is accessible at different levels of practice.

The individual needs clarity and a growth path: a way to understand their strengths, build capability, and bring credibility into the next opportunity. The small or midsize business needs practical improvement without turning the work into a heavy enterprise program. The enterprise needs governance, board agreement, and cross-functional accountability.

Each level needs a different entry point. Micro-learning matters because CX needs accessible entry. Professionals enter at different levels. Some need short, focused learning in customer evidence, service quality, or employee experience. Others need deeper credentials tied to governance and enterprise maturity. A healthy practice creates movement between those levels.

Enterprise certification must include top management. CX at that level belongs to the whole organization. A credible claim to enterprise CX maturity requires leadership connected to the work, board discussion that includes customer outcomes, and an operating system that rewards behavior that builds trust. Standards make that visible. They help the organization see whether CX is a program or a capability.

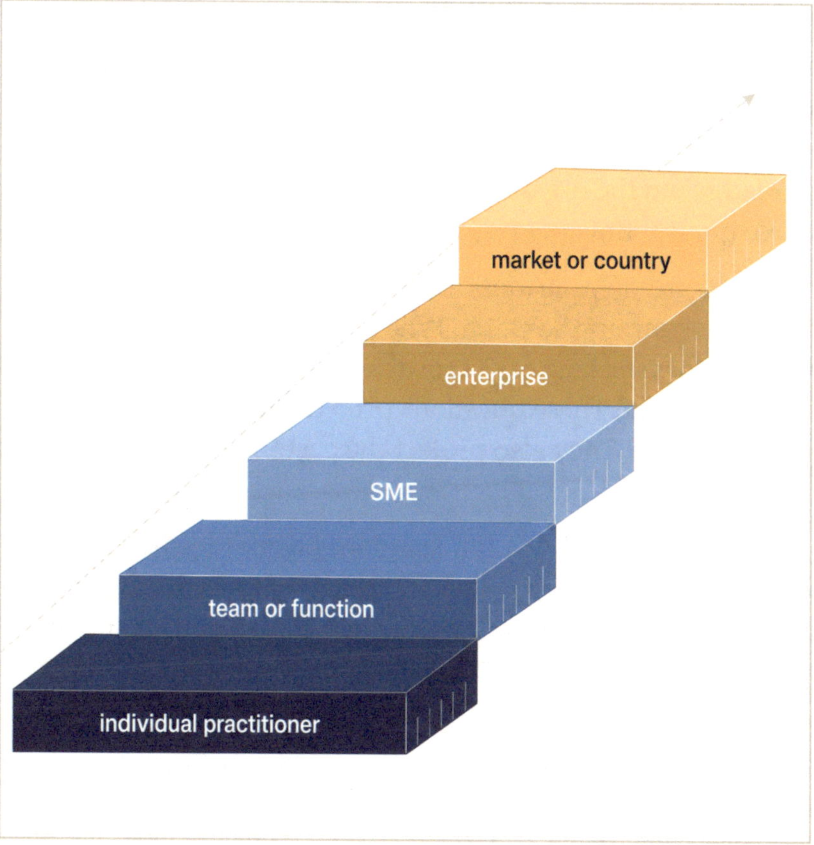


**Figure 17.1** The standards coverage ladder.

Standards create a pathway from individual capability to enterprise credibility.

### Reading Evidence Without Noise

Standards also strengthen how leaders read and use customer evidence. Reviews, search questions, and AI answer results can teach leaders what people are coming to believe. They can also be misread when the organization lacks standards for context, source quality, time period, and population.

A standard helps leaders ask whether the evidence is strong enough to support the claim. Who is speaking? Where did it appear? Does the language repeat across more than one source and population? These questions protect the organization from overconfidence. They also protect the customer from decisions based on noise.

This is where ATLAS$^3$ and standards work together. ATLAS$^3$ helps leaders read movement. Standards help leaders govern the reading. ATLAS$^3$ can show where trust, belief, and customer language are moving. Standards help ensure those findings are used responsibly, consistently, and within appropriate context.

Good standards keep CX from becoming performance language. They require leaders to connect claims to evidence, evidence to decisions, and decisions to customer outcomes. The combination slows leaders down enough to read well, then helps them act with confidence.

Standards speak to the level where the work must improve.

| Level | What it strengthens | What to look for |
|---|---|---|
| Individual practitioner | Skill, language, and credibility | Can the practitioner explain and apply CX with evidence and clarity? |
| Team or function | Shared practice and consistent execution | Can the team connect its work to customer belief and outcomes? |
| SME | Practical improvement and repeatable customer value | Can the business improve experience without unnecessary complexity? |
| Enterprise | Governance, board agreement, and accountability | Can the organization prove CX is a business capability? |
| Market or country | Shared language and service maturity | Can public and private sectors learn from a common experience standard? |

CX needs entry points, growth paths, and enterprise requirements. A single standard cannot serve every need in the same way. The stronger the standard, the more clearly it helps people see what good work looks like at their level.

### Where to Begin

The most practical question is where the organization needs standards most. Does the team lack shared language? Does the company lack a consistent operating rhythm? Does leadership lack a reliable way to judge CX maturity? The answer tells leaders where to begin.

For an individual, that means choosing a pathway that builds real capability. For a team, it means creating shared language around customer evidence and employee enablement. For an enterprise, it means placing CX inside governance, measurement, and board review.

The standard needs to be clear enough to give people a direction and honest enough to show them where they are.

The work becomes teachable. The practice becomes repeatable. The credibility can travel.

---

*The customer benefits because more organizations learn how to build experience with discipline, evidence, and humanity.*

CHAPTER EIGHTEEN

# The Global CX Alliance

The conversation that happens most often at the end of a conference session is the one in the hallway afterward. Two practitioners find each other the way people find someone who speaks their language in a foreign city. The details of industry, country, and title come second. What comes first is recognition.

I have had that conversation in Dubai, in São Paulo, in Seoul. The condition is always the same. A practitioner has been doing this work for years, with a clear way of seeing that their colleagues rarely share. They built their method through fieldwork, failure, and iteration. They may lack language for it. They know it works because they have watched it work, inside organizations that were often encountering those problems for the first time.

They have no peer to take it further.

## The Cost of Isolation

Individual excellence becomes shared knowledge only when something spreads it. I have watched that pattern cost CX for most of its history.

A practitioner who figures out how to read early departure signals from customer language has built a method worth sharing. If that method lives only inside one company, it travels with the person when they leave. The organization that built it loses it. The next practitioner starts without it. The customer who encounters their successor may wait years for the same clarity.

Every new practitioner reinvents the starting point. Every organization that loses a strong CX leader loses a method it never codified. Every market that produces excellent work lacks a reliable way to share what excellent means.

Customer Experience has grown through isolated excellence for most of its history. Individual careers advanced, and companies improved for a time. The discipline itself moved more slowly. The knowledge had nowhere to go that outlasted the person who kept it.

## The Person This Was Built For

In every market where CX is practiced well, there are practitioners who solved problems their organizations were encountering for the first time. I have sat with some of them in Dubai, in Johannesburg, in Seoul, before practitioners agreed on what to call any of it. They were practicing in their own language, in their own markets, under their own conditions. They were already doing the work.

I built the Alliance for that practitioner. The person who has been doing this work in relative isolation and needs language, community, and a path forward.

CX develops fully when the pathway is accessible at every level. The individual needs clarity and a direction: a way to understand their strengths, build capability, and take credibility beyond one company or one market. The small or midsize organization needs practical improvement at a scale it can manage. The enterprise needs governance, board agreement, and cross-functional accountability.

I built the Alliance to serve all three levels because a practice that develops only at the top creates a distance the bottom cannot cross.

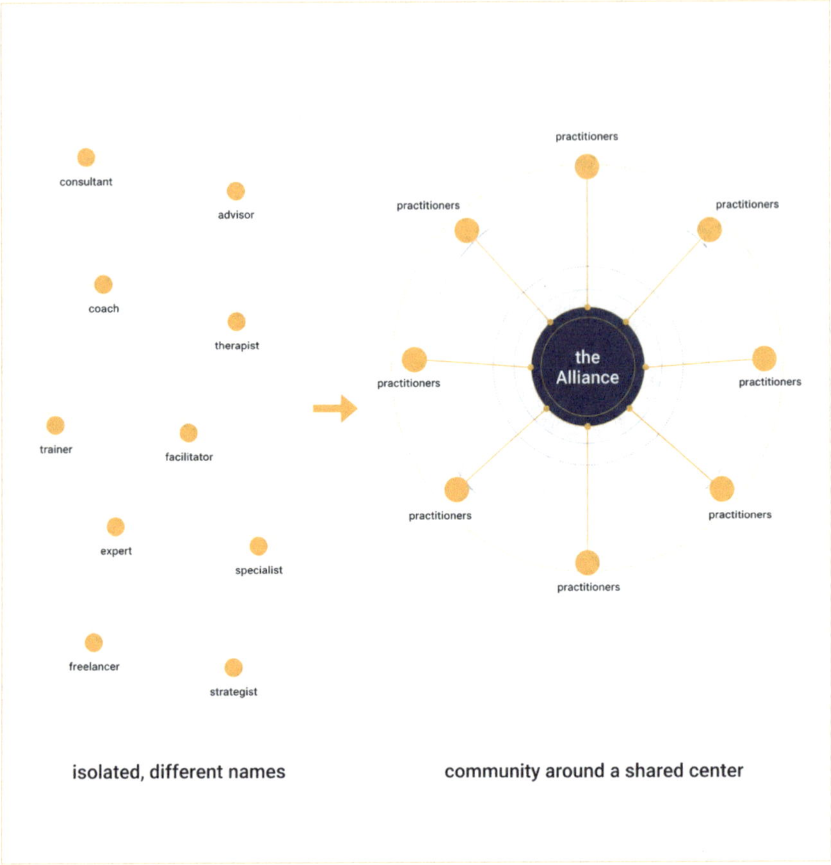


**Figure 18.1** From isolation to community.

The Alliance connects practitioners across markets, disciplines, and career stages who are doing the same work under different names.

### Every Learner Has the Same Value

Every learner has the same value to the harmony of the system.

Mastery differs across practitioners, but the value each brings to the system is the same. A community organized only around advanced practitioners leaves gaps at the entry. A community organized only around learners never raises the standard.

### Where Practitioners Gather

The Alliance operates in markets that differ in language, operating conditions, and customer expectations. Three questions stay constant across every market: what does the customer actually believe, what conditions are shaping that belief, and who is responsible for improving them.

You will find practitioners gathered in community channels organized by discipline, in quarterly sessions across time zones, and in person at events on every continent where the work is happening. Assessment is against a published standard, not reputation or tenure.

The standard asks for demonstrated practice: evidence that the practitioner applied the method under real conditions and produced work that peers can examine. The practitioner who did that work in a difficult real-world situation knows something a written assessment cannot verify. The credential recognizes both kinds of knowing.

### Shrink to Human, ATLAS$^3$, the Alliance

Shrink to Human, ATLAS$^3$, and the Alliance are three expressions of the same commitment.

Shrink to Human is the premise: belief precedes behavior, and the customer decides as a human long before the company can measure what happened. ATLAS$^3$ makes that premise operational at scale, reading customer language, belief movement, and AI answer positions across the populations standard dashboards miss. The Alliance makes it portable: the community, the standards, and the pathways that move CX practice across markets, languages, and career stages.

Three expressions of the same commitment: that human experience in organizations deserves to be made legible, measured honestly, and practiced with discipline.

---

*The hallway conversation kept happening because practitioners had produced more isolated excellence than the practice could move forward. I built the Alliance to give that excellence a structure.*

CHAPTER NINETEEN

# The Learning Pathways

Customer Experience has spent most of its history assigning one title to seven different kinds of work.

The person who traces every organizational recommendation back to verifiable customer language is doing different work from the person who spots where customers slow down before anyone else names it as a problem. The person who translates CX outcomes into the language that survives a budget conversation is doing different work from the person who designs the responsible boundary between automation and human judgment. The titles converge. The work stays separate.

That compression has costs. A practitioner excellent at one kind of seeing gets evaluated against the wrong standard. A hiring leader brings in the wrong person for the need the organization actually has. A company builds a CX function strong in one discipline while the condition the customer is living requires a different one.

I built the Architecture of Practice to make those seven kinds of work distinct. It is the governing structure of the Global CX Alliance, defining what each discipline sees, how it builds, and how practitioners earn the credential.

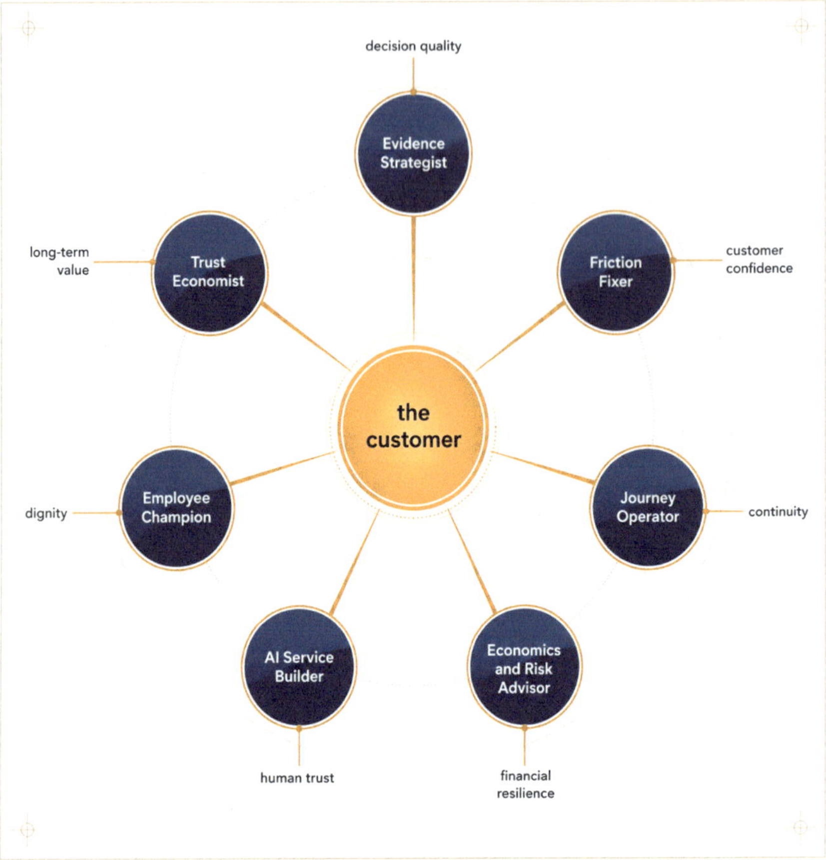


**Figure 19.1** The seven-discipline wheel.

The seven disciplines are a matrix. Every working relationship between them represents a real collaboration the customer depends on.

### What Each Discipline Sees First

At the center of each discipline is a question.

The Evidence Strategist asks: what can this claim actually support? Every organizational decision rests on something either verified or assumed. This discipline separates the two. It protects decisions from errors most organizations discover only after they have acted.

The Friction Fixer's question is simpler and harder: where is the system asking too much of the person? Simpler because it is always findable. Harder because the answer almost always points to something the organization built and believes in.

The Journey Operator asks who owns the experience across stages and handoffs. The customer experiences what happens between moments: the seams, the pauses, the places where continuity breaks and the customer tracks the thread alone.

The Economics and Risk Advisor translates. Customer evidence often comes in a different language from the one organizations use to make decisions. This discipline converts trust conditions into revenue exposure, retention risk, and financial consequence.

The AI Service Builder works on a question CX will be asking for the next decade: what should be automated, augmented, or kept human? Every AI deployment in the customer relationship answers that question, deliberately or by default. This discipline makes the answer deliberate.

The Employee Champion asks what employee condition is shaping the customer outcome. The customer eventually feels what the employee is living. This discipline starts with the employee because that is where the experience begins.

The Trust Economist reads how belief moves across all seven. Belief shifts before behavior. Trust erodes before the metric confirms it. The most consequential changes in a customer relationship happen before the numbers reflect them.

| Archetype | Sees | Builds | Protects |
|---|---|---|---|
| Evidence Strategist | Proof needs | Evidence systems | Decision quality |
| Friction Fixer | Effort | Process relief | Customer confidence |
| Journey Operator | Sequence | Working journeys | Continuity |
| Economics and Risk Advisor | Exposure | Business case | Financial resilience |
| AI Service Builder | Automation moments | Responsible AI service | Human trust |
| Employee Champion | Worker burden | Enablement | Dignity |
| Trust Economist | Belief movement | Trust systems | Long-term value |

## Proven Under Real Conditions

Seven kinds of practice need seven kinds of pathway.

When I designed the credential, the requirement was demonstrated practice. The Global CX Alliance Certified Practitioner has mastery in one primary discipline, demonstrated competence in one secondary discipline, and functional literacy across all seven. Primary mastery means the practitioner applied their method under real organizational conditions and produced work that peers can assess against the rubric.

The credential is renewed through contribution: teaching another practitioner, publishing field work, reviewing a peer's evidence of practice. The practitioner doing live work is always more current than the test that verified them. Knowledge can be tested. Discipline must be demonstrated.

The pathway moves from Learner through Credentialed Practitioner to Certified Practitioner. Fellow is a separate designation, earned through sustained contribution and recognized through nomination and Alliance review.

### Finding Your Discipline

If you have been in CX for any length of time, you probably already know which question you ask first. The Evidence Strategist has been checking the provenance of claims for years before finding language for it. The Friction Fixer noticed the broken step before anyone named it as a problem. The Trust Economist has been reading belief movement while others read scores.

The free archetype assessment at CXArchetype.globalvoicesofcx.com identifies your primary and secondary discipline through ten practice scenarios. If you have been working from one of these disciplines for years, the result feels like recognition rather than revelation.

Each discipline has a playbook, a foundations assessment, and quarterly sessions with practitioners across time zones. If you want to demonstrate the discipline under real conditions, a path to Certified Practitioner exists for you.

**Figure 19.3** Archetype assessment QR code.

**Archetype assessment. globalvoicesofcx.com**

Find out your CX Archetype and join the global alliance.

*The pathway exists to help you prove it.*

FINAL CHAPTER

# Shrink to Human

Shrink to Human.

It means looking inside the scaled system until the person becomes visible again. The customer trying to trust. The employee trying to do good work. The leader trying to understand what is moving before the numbers explain it.

The world will keep scaling. Platforms scale. AI scales. Supply chains scale. Scale is the infrastructure of modern commerce, and it can create extraordinary reach, efficiency, and access. It can also create distance: between the system and the person the system was built to serve.

Shrink to Human is the discipline of closing that distance. It reads the meaning behind the metric, the belief behind the behavior, and the person behind the data point.

## What I Found

The world learned how to scale systems faster than it learned how to understand people.

Belief precedes behavior at every scale. I learned this by watching the distance between what organizations were measuring and what their customers were already living. Customers form trust, doubt, and comparison before the company can measure them. The move is upstream: into customer language before it becomes data, into AI answers that shape first impressions, and into employee conditions that determine what the customer eventually feels.

The 3Rs connect belief to market position. Reputation earns consideration. Reach creates access. Relationships turn trust into continuity. When these three move together, visibility becomes belonging. When they drift, leaders mistake attention for trust, distribution for depth, or growth for health.

The 4Es connect belief to business decision. Economic, Efficient, Emotional, and Empathetic experience each protect a different dimension of the customer relationship. A CX initiative that works only on the easiest dimensions to measure may look strong in the short term while weakening the trust continuity requires.

Employee experience is what the customer eventually feels. Technology either raises human judgment or erases it. Accountability is how belief enters daily decisions instead of remaining a value on a wall.

Standards and pathways allow CX to outlast the people who built it. The practice advances when it can travel.

## When to Shrink to Human

When the dashboard looks stable, shrink to the belief. The score measures what customers reported after a measured interaction. Belief moves earlier: in language, in search, in the quiet comparisons customers make before the company sees them. Stability in the metric can coexist with movement underneath it. The leader's job is to close that distance before the dashboard confirms what the customer already knew.

When the customer goes quiet, shrink to the evidence before the exit. Quiet is information. Customers who stop engaging, stop recommending, or reduce their investment are telling the organization something the formal feedback system misses. That evidence appears in language before it registers in the account data. The organization that reads it early has time to act.

When the organization celebrates scale, shrink to the person who has to live inside it. Every expansion, every automation, every new channel creates a place where the human experience either works or asks too much. Scale earns its strength when the person inside it can trust the company, reach a human when they need one, and feel that the system was built with them in mind.

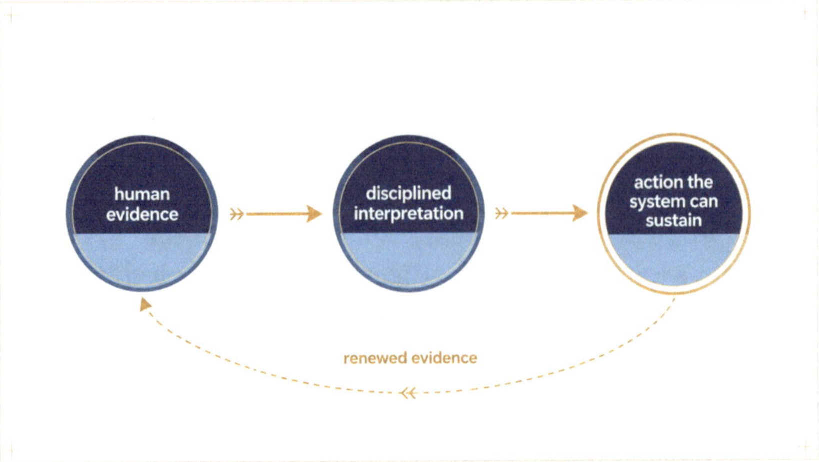


**Figure 20.1** Seeing first.

Seeing first means moving from human evidence to disciplined interpretation, then into action the system can sustain.

## What I Am Asking of You

CX leadership at this level is demanding. It will ask you to see the system and the person at the same time: the metric and the belief behind it, the technology and the dignity it serves, and the business outcome and the human reality beneath it.

It will ask you to grow others in this discipline. The next generation of CX will be built by practitioners who can read belief before behavior, govern AI with named accountability, and take credibility across markets and operating environments.

| Commitment | What it means in practice | What it strengthens |
|---|---|---|
| See belief before behavior | Read what customers are coming to believe before the outcome appears | Earlier judgment |
| Read evidence outside the dashboard | Include reviews, search questions, and AI answer results | Wider visibility |
| Protect employee dignity | Give employees clarity, authority, and forward movement | Human delivery |
| Govern AI with named owners | Assign accountable people to every customer-facing AI system | Trustworthy scale |
| Build the matrix | Make every function responsible for the belief it helps create | Shared ownership |
| Use standards as pathways | Help practitioners grow with shared language and credible credentials | CX maturity |

## The Work Continues

CX leadership is the discipline of keeping human belief visible inside systems built to process at speed.

My purpose is to help people and systems understand each other at scale. I have pursued that purpose across thirty years, forty countries, and more than a hundred and fifty conversations that became the foundation of this practice. What I found is that the organizations that earn loyalty and the practitioners who sustain careers share one quality: they see the person before they see the system. They keep that view even when the system grows large enough to make the person hard to find.

Customer Experience is where belief, service, and human dignity meet at scale. When organizations do this work well, daily life becomes easier for the people who depend on their systems. When practitioners build this capability with rigor, the discipline becomes worthy of the trust it asks for.

The world will keep scaling.

The work is to make that scale more worthy of people.

---

*Shrink to Human.*

EPILOGUE

# Contributing Authors

## Ladislau Batalha · Gregório Uglioni
## Camila Ferreira · Cristiani Oliveira

GLOBAL CX ALLIANCE · FOUNDING MEMBERS

My journey has spanned more than forty nations and included deep discussions with upwards of 150 practitioners. Throughout these encounters, my focus remained steadfast on uncovering the underlying logic, methodology, and fundamental convictions that drive their work.

During the formation of the Global CX Alliance, I was pleasantly surprised by the profound insights I gained regarding the human element of customer experience. The passions of these individuals extend far beyond the technical frameworks they utilize.

I extend my deepest thanks for their invaluable contributions to both this publication and the Global CX Alliance.

Chapter Eleven, Employee Experience Is Where CX Becomes Human First, was inspired by Ladislau. He infuses his work with a sense of pure delight. After hearing about his journey from

Paris to Lisbon, where he lost his luggage across three different nations just to keep a promise to a new community member without ever complaining, I finally found the perspective I had been seeking.

Gregório's lifelong commitment to sharing his expertise and preventing others from stumbling over the same hurdles he faced helped shape Chapter Fourteen, Belief Becomes Repeatable Through Systems. His daily practice of selfless generosity was exactly the foundation I needed for that chapter.

Moving from the financial sector in Brazil to the customer experience field in the United States, Camila carries the richness of both worlds with her. Rather than merely translating between these cultures, she has integrated them, providing the clarity I needed for Chapter Ten, The 4Es.

From Cristiani, I learned that being transparent about what you haven't yet mastered is a deep sign of respect for those relying on your results. This insight was instrumental in refining Chapter Four, Customer Evidence Outside the Dashboard.

The contributions of these four individuals have not only expanded my vision but have profoundly impacted my life.

**Dennis Wakabayashi**

*The Global Voice of CX · Founder, Global CX Alliance*

CONTRIBUTING AUTHOR · FRICTION FIXER

# Ladislau Batalha

*Customer Experience and Operations Leader · Founder and Managing Director, Lab Experience · Chair, CX Summit Lisbon 2026*

*Customers leave when it becomes harder than it should be.*

Customers often form opinions before a company is even aware of them. The review, the message to a peer, the comment posted in a forum at eleven at night: specific, time-stamped, and already part of the public record. By the time the internal report flags the issue, the signal has been developing for months.

I see this every day from inside operations. Whether working with a contact center in Dubai, a banking team in Lisbon, or a government service organization in the Gulf, the pattern repeats. The agent hears what is happening on Tuesday morning. Six weeks later, the report confirms it. By that point, the organization is managing the outcome of something it never saw coming.

Twenty-five years across banking, government, aviation, and hospitality taught me something specific about that early signal. It does not just arrive before the report. It arrives with an address.

Every phrase the customer uses points to a location inside the operation. Having to call back three times is a handoff. Nobody being able to find the record is a knowledge access issue. Giving up and canceling is where decision rights stopped. A patient receives excellent care, but their family sits for two hours in a room with no wifi and no water, and later writes that the hospital visit was bad. The experience was defined too narrowly. It left out part of what the family lived through. The customer is not describing a sentiment. They are describing the step, the channel, what they tried, and what happened. That is a map.

The Friction Audit follows the map, identifying where customer effort spikes and using that language as the signal. It names the cause specifically, not generally. Remove the cause by changing the system, not by asking the customer to do more.

Most organizations are good at locating. Many are capable of naming. The third move is the one skill that requires real commitment because it means changing something the organization has built. The hold queue is too long, so a tool is added. The customer navigates the tool but does not reach a resolution and returns to the hold queue. The friction changed shape. The customer's request did not decrease. The report will still show a deflection. The fix that transfers the issue looks like progress in the data, but feels like more effort to the person living it.

What I want to share with anyone reading this is a single habit: read the customer signal twice. Once to consider what was felt. Once to understand where it happened.

Founding Member, Global CX Alliance · Friction Fixer · Lab Experience, United Arab Emirates, Brazil, Portugal

ladislau@globalvoicesofcx.com · labexperience.cx

CONTRIBUTING AUTHOR · JOURNEY OPERATOR

# Gregório Uglioni

*Customer Experience and Transformation Advisor · Associate Partner, Forward Partners AG · Host, The CX Goalkeeper*

*Customers know if the program is working before leadership does.*

I ask myself every morning how I can positively impact people that day.

That question has a specific origin. I spent ten years in financial services running transformation programs before moving into a hospital. In banking, you work with products, portfolios, and service levels. In a hospital, you work with health. One life. One body. The question stops being abstract when the stakes are that direct.

What I learned is that a patient does not need to explain what changed to demonstrate whether it has changed. You see it in how they move through the building. Whether they ask questions or stay silent. Whether they trust the system to work for them or navigate carefully around it. The felt experience is the evidence. It arrives before any survey confirms it.

Beliefs are established before an organization has the means to measure them. And whether a transformation works becomes evident in people's experience long before a leadership report identifies it.

This is what I have come to understand about the programs I have seen sustain and those that dissolve. The ones that dissolved were often well designed. The strategy was right. The milestones were clear. But the outcome depended on individuals, and when those individuals moved, the outcome moved with them. The consultant left before the flowers grew. I know, because I have been that consultant.

The programs that last are built differently. The outcome lives in the system, not the person. Decision rights are built into how the work runs. Evidence is defined at each stage so teams can see whether the work is taking hold without needing the person who designed it to be present. The executive sponsor can move on. The budget can reset. The program keeps running because the system was designed to maintain the belief, not depend on the person.

The CX Goalkeeper sees the whole pitch. From behind the game, you can see what the players in the middle cannot. You can see where the system is working and where it is about to break. Name what you see and give it to the people who can act.

The question I ask now, before anything launches, is this: if every person on the team changed roles tomorrow, what would keep running? Write down what survives. What survives is what you actually built. What requires you or the sponsor to stay is what still needs work.

The system has to maintain the belief when the person is not there.

Why should you make the same mistake I made? Learn from it. Then go make the mistakes that belong to your situation. Those are the ones worth making.

Founding Member, Global CX Alliance · Journey Operator · DACH and the European Union

gregorio@globalvoicesofcx.com · Host, The CX Goalkeeper

CONTRIBUTING AUTHOR · ECONOMICS AND RISK ADVISOR

# Camila Ferreira

*Global Business Strategist · Founder, Limitless Talks · Co-author, Long Live CX*

*Alone, you grow. Together, you become limitless.*

Leaders make decisions before they see the full signal.

I have watched this from two sides of the table. My first ten years were in finance. I learned the language executives use when real money is at stake, the questions they actually ask when a proposal reaches them, and the order in which they need to hear things before trust forms around a number.

When I moved into customer experience, I realized the same decision problem appears from a different angle. Organizations make CX investments on internal data, internal belief, and internal metrics. The signal that exists outside those systems, in reviews, in forums, in AI-mediated discovery, in what customers say to each other when the company is not present, is often not part of the picture. By the time it enters the conversation, the commitment is already made, and the investment is defending itself rather than building.

My own professional background informs the financial translation I provide. While many CX professionals possess fluency in journey metrics, satisfaction scores, and internal functional terminology, this internal vocabulary often fails to resonate with a CFO. It lacks the endurance required for budget discussions; if you cannot justify an investment in the language of decision-makers, the CX function's defense will go unheard.

My tenure leading Uber Eats during the pandemic reinforced this reality. In that high-stakes environment, there was no separation between financial and customer outcomes; they converged simultaneously with immediate consequences. I learned that you cannot effectively serve customers while disregarding economic realities, nor can you protect the economics while ignoring the customer experience. This necessity transformed what once seemed like two distinct dialects into a single, unified language of business.

A churn rate improvement is a revenue protection story. A reduction in support contacts is a cost-to-serve story. A customer who deepens product adoption is a revenue-per-customer story. Every CX outcome has a financial translation. The leader who can move between the two fluently is the one whose voice still matters when the decision is made.

I want every reader to adopt the habit of translation. Identify your most frequent metric and draft a single sentence linking its improvement to a specific line on a financial statement, such as lowering churn risk, reducing the cost per contact, or retaining revenue. If you can produce that sentence in thirty seconds, you have achieved translation; if it takes a paragraph to reach a value, your work remains incomplete.

Clarity makes human capability limitless. That clarity begins by identifying the correct language and providing the necessary evidence when a decision is on the line.

Founding Member, Global CX Alliance · Economics and Risk Advisor · East Coast USA and Brazil

camila@globalvoicesofcx.com · Founder, Limitless Talks

CONTRIBUTING AUTHOR · EVIDENCE STRATEGIST

# Cristiani Oliveira

*Customer Experience Researcher and Evidence Strategist · Partner and COO, Lab Experience · Executive Architect, CX Summit Lisbon*

*Data-driven decision-making is a leadership discipline.*

A customer experience claim is only as strong as the evidence behind it.

I work at the layer where that statement becomes structural. The organizations I engage with face review from boards, regulators, and AI-mediated discovery systems that compress what a company claims about its customer experience into a summary a buyer reads before speaking to anyone in the organization. Whatever form the review takes, the claim has to survive it. Leaders hire me to find the truth, even when it is not beautiful.

The challenge I find in nearly every engagement is not the absence of data. Organizations have more data than they know how to use. The challenge is that a claim that began in a specific review, written by a specific customer on a specific date, becomes more powerful than it really is. It travels as knowledge. It lives as an assumption. The difference between an objective method and a subjective one is easy to lose once a claim is in motion.

Inside an internal meeting, that claim can survive on trust. Take it into a board review, a regulatory examination, or an AI-mediated summary, and trust is not the standard. Provenance is.

To practice evidence architecture is to master the art of preserving the narrative path. Every conclusion must be linked back to the specific customer voice that initiated it; we ensure the language, timing, and channel remain intact. By defining the sample, its constraints, and its importance, we create the traceability necessary for findings to withstand rigorous review. This ensures that causation is never confused with mere correlation.

The inclusion of the external record is vital because it highlights the discrepancy between organizational metrics and actual customer decision-making. While internal data shows what a company chooses to track, external sources such as customer research, reviews, forum discussions, AI-mediated searches, and peer recommendations reveal the reality of the customer experience.

These two perspectives do not always align. When a gap exists, it represents the most critical insight: the distance between the experience a brand intended to design and the one customers truly live. This crucial distinction is rarely apparent when relying solely on internal data.

I want to leave you with a specific habit: before any findings influence a strategic discussion, ask three questions. How many customers said it? Through which channel? On what date? If you possess these three answers, you have evidence. If the justification sounds like "based on our years of experience" or "the general customer sentiment is," you are dealing with a belief. While such beliefs might be accurate or helpful, they do not constitute evidence. Choosing between evidence and assumptions ultimately defines the level of risk an organization is prepared to take.

The objective is to clarify the vision as much as possible to ensure decisions are well-informed without stalling progress, as most choices occur before the complete picture emerges. Ultimately, the decision itself is what matters; research by itself does not alter results. For leadership, the true test lies in turning insights into meaningful business actions.

Founding Member, Global CX Alliance · Evidence Strategist · Lisbon based, Europe, and Africa

cristiani@globalvoicesofcx.com · Executive Architect, CX Summit Lisbon

# About the Author

## Dennis Wakabayashi, The Global Voice of CX

He has sat with contact center agents in South Africa, and with founders, advisors, and designers across Vietnam, the Emirates, and Portugal. Thirty years and more than twenty countries, and the same thing keeps showing up: we have learned to scale systems faster than we have learned to understand the people inside them.

He built ATLAS$^3$ to close that distance. It reads customer language, search behavior, and the answers AI returns, across the people most organizations never hear from. He founded and chairs the Global CX Alliance and leads Brave Ah!, the agency that reads what customers write rather than what companies write about themselves.

The method has been tested in real-world settings. He has led customer experience strategy for brands such as McDonald's, Wells Fargo, FedEx, AT&T, and Intuit. Leaders, governors, and royalty in more than 120 countries have asked for his read. He has keynoted on nearly every continent, and close to a million people follow the work, more than 500,000 of them on YouTube.

The fieldwork has not stopped. *CX in the Wild*, his in-person research podcast, is in its eleventh season and has had over 100 practitioner conversations. *Shrink to Human* is what those conversations add up to, his third book after *Long Live CX* (2024) and *Laying Golden Eggs* (2021).

He has taught digital marketing at the University of Wisconsin–Madison and CX Principles courses for O'Reilly Media. He serves as an international CX judge and chairman for leading industry events. *Campaign US* named him one of its Top 40 Over 40 digital marketers. He holds two Webby Awards, ranks among the Top 50 CX People of the Decade, and made LinkedIn's Top 200 Voices in Customer Service Worldwide for 2026.

# How to Work with Brave Ah!

*We begin by listening to the people you serve, and the people you want to reach.*

braveah.com carla@braveah.com

HOW WE WORK

## We start by listening

The people you serve, and the people deciding whether to choose you, talk in public every day. There is a great deal to learn by listening.

### We listen

ATLAS[3] reads two years of what your market has said in public, in the words buyers use.

### We plan

What it finds becomes your plan for the year: one objective, the goals that reach it, and the work that moves them. Built on the evidence.

### We deliver

We produce and publish the work each month, then report what moved. What we make is yours, and it keeps working without us.

WHAT BUILDS TRUST

# What makes buyers choose you

A buyer forms an opinion about you long before they talk to you. Two things shape it: how your reputation forms, and what your experience delivers. We name both in seven parts, drawn from *Shrink to Human*, so you can see them and move them.

## How your reputation forms: the 3Rs

### Reputation

What people say about you when you are not in the room.

### Reach

How far that reputation travels, and whether the right people find you.

### Relationships

Whether the buyers you win stay, and bring others.

## What your experience delivers: the 4Es

| Economic | Efficient | Emotional | Empathetic |
|---|---|---|---|
| Whether the price feels worth it. | Whether you are easy to buy from and easy to use. | How a buyer feels dealing with you. | Whether a buyer feels understood as a person. |

When the seven line up, a buyer chooses you with less hesitation. Together they produce Trust, the one goal the whole year works to move. Whichever way you start, the work moves these seven and grows your Trust.

WHERE TO BEGIN

# Four ways to start

The Research and the Quarter are one path: the Research sets your year, and the Quarter delivers it. The Project is a single piece of work on its own. The Conversation is the way in when you are not sure.

01

### Start with the Research

Sets your year. We read your market and build the plan the rest of the work follows.

02

### Start with a Quarter

Delivers your year, ninety days at a time. It builds on the Research.

03

### Start with a Project

One piece of work on its own, when you have a single need.

04

### Start with a Conversation

The way in when you are not sure. It costs nothing.

WAY 1

# Start with the Research

The Research is the foundation, and the rest of the work builds on it. It comes from ATLAS$^3$, our proprietary AgenticCX research and the only platform of its kind in the world. ATLAS$^3$ reads two years of what your market has said in public, finds where you stand on the seven, and turns it into the plan for your year.

## How it runs

1. **Intake session**

   You share what you know about your customers, your market, and where you stand now. The account lead writes down what they hear. The research starts from there.

2. **Research runs**

   We read what people say about you across public channels, map the competitors who show up, and record the words they use for your category.

3. **Findings review**

   The account lead walks you through the findings, line by line: where buyers are forming opinions, which competitors are gaining ground and where, and what language people use that your content does not yet reflect.

4. **Planning session**

   Together we set one objective and write the goals, each with a starting number, a target, and a date. The work connects to those goals, and we set what we score and how often.

5. **Plan delivered**

   We design four quarterly campaigns from the plan you approved, and we write up your buyer profiles. The year of direction is yours, whether or not the work continues.

## What you learn

You learn where you stand on each of the seven against the average of your top five competitors, from where you start to now, and what it takes to move. Trust is what the seven produce together, and it is the goal the year points at.

## Where you show up when a buyer looks

When a buyer looks for what you do, you are at one of five steps, from not there at all to the obvious choice. These five steps come from *Shrink to Human*.

| | |
|---|---|
| **Ignored** | You do not come up at all. |
| **Mentioned** | Your name comes up, with little behind it. |
| **Compared** | You are weighed against the alternatives. |
| **Preferred** | You are recommended, with reasons. |
| **Default** | You are the obvious choice. |

## What you receive

### Baseline Intelligence Report

The findings, across the public channels we covered.

### Buyer Profiles (2 to 3)

Built from the words people used in public.

### Annual Plan

Your objective, the goals that reach it, and the work that moves them. One document, built on the evidence.

### 12-Month Campaign Architecture

Four quarters mapped to the plan, ready to brief.

### Competitor Map

Which competitors show up, where, and in what language.

### Buyer Language Library

The words people use, by topic and by stage of the decision.

WAY 2

# Start with a Quarter

You have a direction and a budget, and you need a team and a system to run them. A Quarter is a ninety-day campaign built on the Research. Every month's work moves the seven, and the report shows you where Trust and the rest moved.

## The year in four phases

**Q1**

### Establish

Build the first content from the research. Mark where you start.

**Q2**

### Amplify

Take the content to more of the right people. Go deeper where it worked.

**Q3**

### Convert

Help buyers move from considering you to choosing you. Build proof.

**Q4**

### Compound

Keep what you built, and keep adding to it. Set up the next year.

## How each month runs

**WEEK 1**

### Plan

We read the market, set the focus, and plan the work.

**WEEK 2**

### Build

We build the long pieces first, then the short ones.

**WEEK 3**

### Approve and publish

You approve. The work goes live.

**WEEK 4**

### Publish and measure

The rest goes live, and results start to come in.

WAY 2

## What you get each quarter

A quarter can look like this. What we find each month decides the actual mix.

### Long-Form Articles (3)

1,500 to 2,000 words each. Your site. One per sprint.

### Executive Bylines (3)

800 to 1,000 words. LinkedIn. Written from the language people use.

### Short-Form Social Posts (24)

Image and caption. LinkedIn, Instagram, X. Eight per sprint.

### Short-Form Video Clips (9)

9:16, 30 to 60 seconds. LinkedIn and Instagram. Three per sprint.

### Email Newsletter Features (3)

200 to 300 words. To your list. One per sprint.

### Pull-Quote Graphics (9)

Branded graphics. All social channels. Three per sprint.

### Press Releases (3)

Standard format. Wire and your newsroom. One per sprint.

### Performance Reports (3)

The seven scored against your category, with a short summary for leadership.

### Quarterly Review Deck

Results measured against the brief. The next quarter's brief comes from it.

WAY 3

# Start with a Project

You have one specific need: a podcast that captures your thinking, a video for a launch, an executive presence built over time, an event covered and reused, or a piece of original research. A project moves a specific part of the seven: your reputation, your reach, or the proof behind you. You bring the brief, we scope it, and the work is yours.

### How it runs

1. **Scope session**
   Together we write down the deliverables, formats, channels, timeline, and how work gets approved. You approve the scope before work starts.
2. **Production brief**
   What gets built, who owns it, and when it is due, against the timeline you agreed to.
3. **Production and review**
   We build against the brief and share drafts at each review. Revisions finish before final approval.
4. **Final delivery**
   We deliver the approved work in final format, with source files and usage rights written down.

WAY 3

## Example project: a six-episode podcast

### Show Strategy Document

Show name, tagline, audience, episode format. Week 1.

### Show Artwork

3000 x 3000 RGB. Submitted to all platforms. Week 2.

### Recorded Episodes (6)

WAV master and MP3. Apple, Spotify, YouTube.

### Show Notes and Transcripts (6)

Timestamped notes and full transcript. Your site.

### Audiogram Clips (18)

Three per episode. 9:16, 60 seconds. LinkedIn and Instagram.

### Short-Form Video Clips (12)

Two per episode. 30 to 60 seconds. LinkedIn.

### LinkedIn Posts (12)

Two per episode. Image and caption.

### Email Announcements (6)

One per episode. To your list.

### Season Recap Article

1,500 words across the full series. Your site, at the close.

WAY 4

# Start with a Conversation

You are not sure which way fits. The first conversation is a working session. You describe what you are facing. We tell you where you likely stand on the seven, what would move your Trust fastest, and what the first piece of work should be. You leave with a point of view and a place to start, whether or not you go further.

## Who this is for

### CX leader

You have the ideas from the book. Your organization does not yet have the production to act on them at the level the work asks for.

### Marketing executive

Your team is producing content. You want a clear picture of whether it reaches the right buyer at the right point in the decision.

### Brand or product leader

You have a launch, a repositioning, or a competitive response that needs to move. You need a team that keeps pace with the decision.

### Government or institution leader

You answer for how a population understands and uses the systems built to serve them. The distance between the promise and the experience can be measured.

### Independent professional

You are building a body of work and a presence that is yours and travels with you when you change roles.

## What you leave with

A clear picture of where you stand in your category, the first step we would take, and a written recommendation. You owe nothing to receive it.

WHAT YOU KEEP

# Everything we make is yours

The work is a relationship, and all of it stays with you. When an engagement ends, you keep the plan, the research, the work, and the record of how it was done. The program is built to run without us.

### The plan and the research

Your plan, the findings, the buyer language, and the competitor map.

### The work

Every article, video, episode, post, and report made during the engagement.

### The system

The process and the record, so the program keeps running on its own.

carla@braveah.com braveah.com

**Brands. Institutions. Governments. Any language. Any time zone. Any scale.**

Made in the USA
Monee, IL
05 November 2026

67810990R00107